A CREATIVE STEP-BY-STEP GUIDE TO

GARDEN
DESIGN

A CREATIVE STEP-BY-STEP GUIDE TO

GARDEN
DESIGN

Author
Yvonne Rees

Photographer
Neil Sutherland

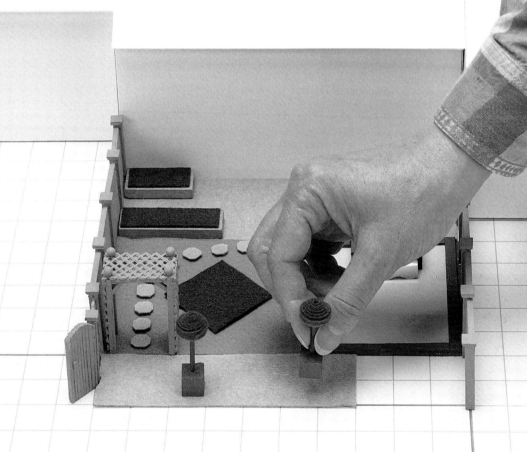

WHITECAP BOOKS

CLB 3311
This edition published in 1995 by
Whitecap Books Ltd., 351 Lynn Avenue
North Vancouver, B.C., Canada V7J 2C4
© 1995 CLB Publishing, Godalming, Surrey, England
All rights reserved. No part of this publication may be
reproduced, stored in a retrieval system, or transmitted
in any form or by any means, electronic, mechanical,
photocopying, recording or otherwise, without written
permission of the publisher and copyright holder.
Printed in Singapore
ISBN 1-55110-177-7

Credits

Edited and designed: Ideas into Print
Photographs: Neil Sutherland
Photo location: Bridgemere Garden World, Cheshire
Typesetting: Ideas into Print and Ash Setting and Printing
Production Director: Gerald Hughes
Production: Ruth Arthur, Sally Connolly, Neil Randles

THE AUTHOR

Yvonne Rees has been involved with garden design and
maintenance, both on a practical level as a gardener and as
a designer, for more than 20 years. For several years,
Yvonne worked in London's Chelsea Physic Garden, one
of the oldest surviving collections of herbs and rare plants,
but she currently writes, lectures and broadcasts on all
aspects of gardening and garden design. Hcr countless
articles and books have been published in many languages
around the world.

THE PHOTOGRAPHER

Neil Sutherland has more than 25 years experience in a
wide range of photographic fields, including still-life,
portraiture, reportage, natural history, cookery, landscape
and travel. His work has been published in countless books
and magazines throughout the world.

Half-title page: A stylish wooden bench sets off a bank
of cottage garden plants to perfection.

Title page: Creating simple models helps you to visualize
your ideas in miniature before you turn them into reality.
Here, bay trees in containers introduce a classic note to an
informal patio area at the bottom of the garden.

Copyright page: Using pots in the border enables you to
introduce new colors and shapes as the seasons change.

CONTENTS

Part One

PLANNING YOUR GARDEN

You can create a beautiful and successful garden without employing an expensive landscape architect - the key is good planning. By following a few practical pointers and adding a little personal flair and imagination, good planning can transform your raw new plot, untamed jungle or cramped and gloomy backyard into your dream garden in a single season. The first step is to get to know exactly what you have: the size, shape and orientation of the site, plus any existing major features. The aim is then to emphasize the best points and hide or disguise the bad ones. But before you even start to consider the practicalities of this, it is important that you have a clear idea of the style of garden and the kind of features you are keen to include in the final plan. This will make decisions much easier during the planning stage and produce a finished garden with cohesion and balance. The first part of this book takes you easily and logically through the stages of planning a garden. The ideas here are only suggestions; it is much more important that you have fun with your own.

Left: A weeping pear tree at the focal point of a formal garden.   *Above:* Hostas are superb architectural plants.

First thoughts

So where do you start? Before you rush out and start digging and planting, take a tip from the professionals and experiment on paper first. Begin by sizing up the site. Measure around the perimeter and draw up a plan to scale on graph paper. Now you can see what you have to work with, you can mark in any existing features and indicate the particularly sunny or shady areas. This is important when choosing certain plants and features. Now before you go any further, draw up a list of all the elements you would like to see included in your ideal garden: maybe a fine lawn, a patio area, traditional flower beds, an ornamental pool, and so on. There might not be room for all of them - although most features can be scaled down to suit - but this will help you shortlist those you consider the most important. You can get clever ideas to stimulate your imagination from all kinds of sources: photographs in books, television gardening programs, annual shows and exhibitions or local gardens open to the public. At this point you can have fun making scale models of your new garden features to give you a real impression of how it is going to look. Or you could use toy modelling bricks or cut pictures from gardening catalogs and magazines to simulate the effect you are aiming for. It is worth spending a few hours at your local garden center, not only to absorb garden ideas, but also to see what features and materials are readily available. Now is also a good time to take note of the cost, as this may affect your plans. Even a small item might inspire you and trigger off an idea for a feature or a total look for the garden. If you can develop a theme for the whole garden, or even a part of it, you will achieve a far more balanced and professional looking result with everything, even the plants, chosen to fit in.

Making models

The models featured in the first part of this book are easy to create from simple materials such as paper, card, felt and balsa wood. The trellis panels are cut from sheets of perforated plastic made for tapestry. The ornamental spheres on the top of fence posts and arches are simply painted map pins. The illusion of water is easy to achieve by sticking clear adhesive plastic over blue paper. Model shops can supply a wide range of paints - the ones that dry to a matt finish are best - and other materials that you can use to make attractive and useful models.

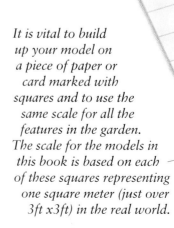

The model houses are purposely neutral in color and style to avoid drawing attention away from the garden design. In the real world, the size, style and position of houses have a great influence over the gardens they overlook.

It is vital to build up your model on a piece of paper or card marked with squares and to use the same scale for all the features in the garden. The scale for the models in this book is based on each of these squares representing one square meter (just over 3ft x3ft) in the real world.

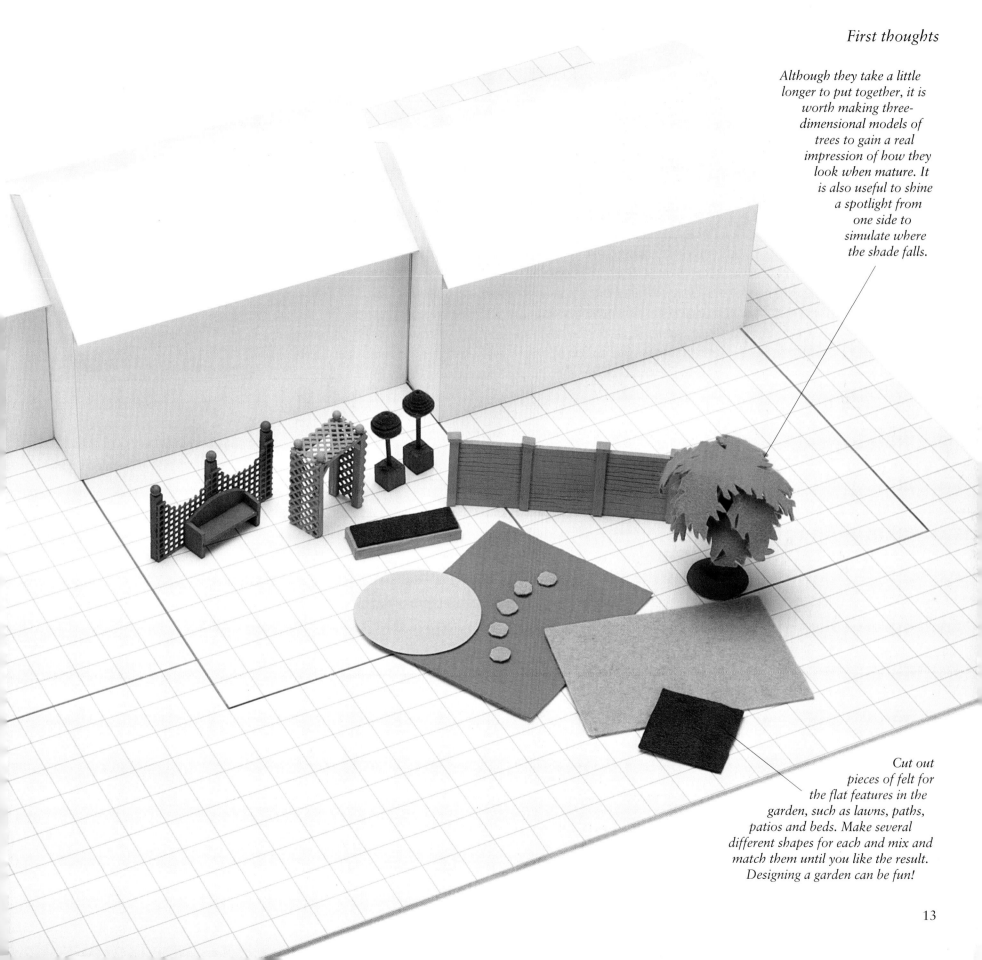

Although they take a little longer to put together, it is worth making three-dimensional models of trees to gain a real impression of how they look when mature. It is also useful to shine a spotlight from one side to simulate where the shade falls.

Cut out pieces of felt for the flat features in the garden, such as lawns, paths, patios and beds. Make several different shapes for each and mix and match them until you like the result. Designing a garden can be fun!

Choosing your boundaries

The boundaries of the garden plot should be your first consideration when planning the total look and style of your hoped-for scheme. They are easily overlooked in the excitement of planning a garden, but what goes on around the perimeter is not as unobtrusive and irrelevant as you might think; in fact it can have a considerable influence on the final effect and should be designed in conjunction with other major features. Most likely, you will have inherited some kind of wall, fence or trellis, which may or may not be suitable. Replacement can be expensive, so you might have to compromise by redesigning certain areas at first, say around key spaces such as the patio. If you find the effect totally unacceptable, resort to some kind of disguise or cover-up, such as inexpensive trellis, climbing plants or decorative screens. First decide whether the structure is doing the job for which it is intended; a lightweight post and rail fence is fine where you want to appreciate a fine view beyond the garden, but for privacy or shelter you need something more substantial. Before constructing or changing any permanent structure, check exactly which boundaries you or your neighbor are responsible for and make sure there are no local planning restrictions on size and style.

Below: Timber fence posts and panels are available in various styles. Allow the timber to weather, or stain or paint it to suit your scheme.

Boundary walls

A wall is more expensive and time-consuming to build, but it is maintenance-free, durable and offers better security for vulnerable gardens. Old, second-hand bricks produce an instantly mellow effect, but new bricks come in many colors and shades for creating interesting patterns. Alternatively, cover the wall with climbing plants fixed to special hooks and wires or trained over a detachable trellis. An old and dominant existing wall often benefits from being painted white to add a little light.

Below: A hedge takes longer to establish, but makes an attractive, natural background for other features.

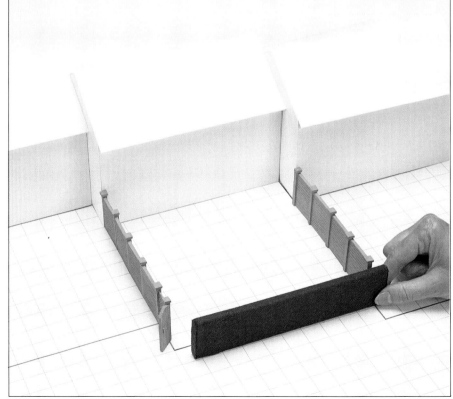

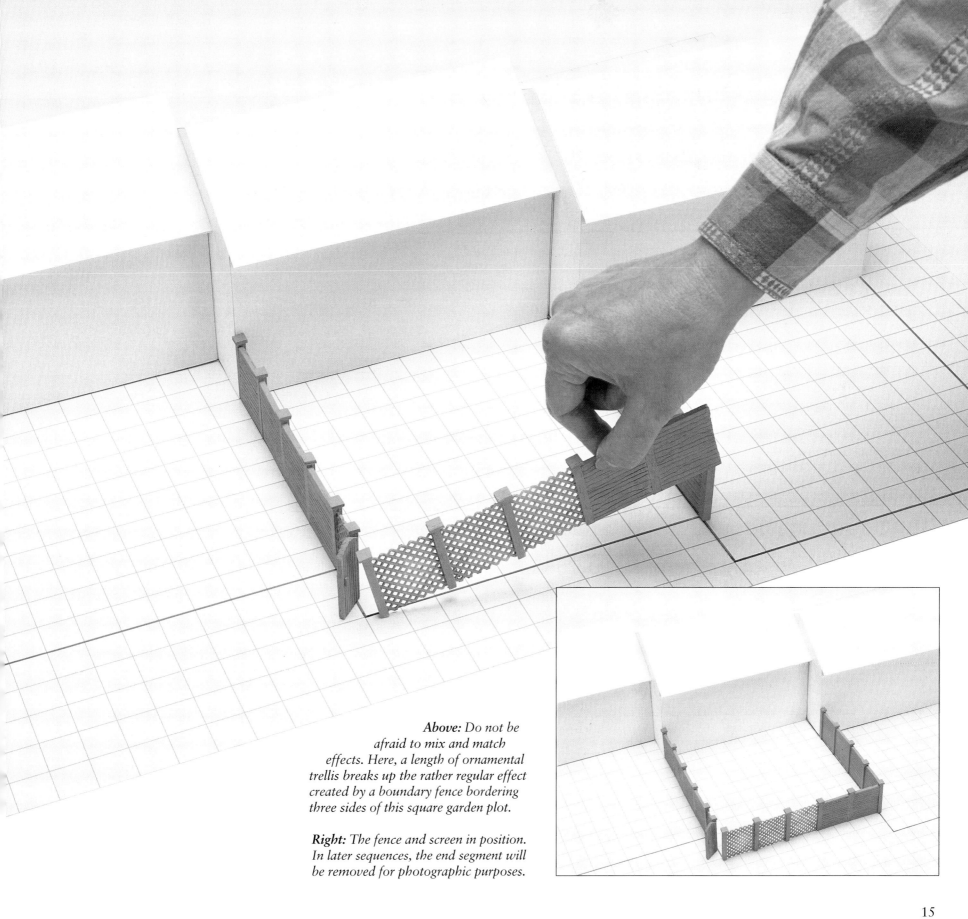

Above: *Do not be afraid to mix and match effects. Here, a length of ornamental trellis breaks up the rather regular effect created by a boundary fence bordering three sides of this square garden plot.*

Right: *The fence and screen in position. In later sequences, the end segment will be removed for photographic purposes.*

Boundary options

Fences come in many types and styles that vary not only in looks, but also in strength and suitability. Whichever you choose, the panels will only be as sturdy as the posts they are fixed to and these should be well bedded in the ground and preferably bolted to special concrete fencing posts. You can bed timber posts directly into concrete, which is more attractive but less durable, as the timber rots below ground level. Or you can insert them into metal fencing spikes, which can be difficult to get into stony ground. The simplest, most open type of boundary fence is ranch-style, which consists of two or three horizontal rails between the posts. It is in no way animal-proof and affords no privacy, but it does mark a boundary without impeding a fine view. A wicket fence, where regular upright palings are fixed to the rails, will keep dogs out of the garden but, like rustic panels, is not completely private. For this you need a close-boarded or feather-boarded type of fence. These can be quite ornamental with the top trimmed into a shaped profile and matching posts with decorative caps. Walls offer a similarly wide range of options using brick, natural stone or blocks. Walls need good foundations; take this into account when estimating costs. Height, width and pattern can all affect strength and stability. Bricks are particularly versatile and available in a wide range of colors, which can be used to create bands and patterns. The bricks themselves can be arranged into patterns and designs, such as basketweave, although they will need extra reinforcement to compensate for the aligning vertical joints.

Above: This screen made from compressed branches provides a very natural-looking backdrop for an informal planting scheme packed with interesting foliage shapes and colors.

Left: Clipped evergreen hedges conjure up a timeless, old-fashioned feel, especially when teamed with features such as traditional herbaceous borders, classic pillars and a tumble of white wisteria, as here.

Left: Unexpected color can work well; this dark-blue stained trellis complements the massed greens of dense planting and has natural panel insets to lighten the effect.

Right: In a garden where plants predominate, this rough wooden fence is sufficient to mark the boundary and in spring is barely visible above a sea of narcissus.

Below: If privacy is not an issue, a simple wicket fence is smart yet informal. This one has instant country appeal, with its full head of honeysuckle and cottage flowers.

Rough, unfinished timber and hasty-looking construction is half the charm of this informal fence.

White-painted fences require regular maintenance. Plastic ones are also available.

Below: A dry stone wall needs time and skill to construct successfully, but produces a wonderfully natural mellow effect in an informal garden, especially once it is covered in plants.

Left: Sometimes it is better to site the patio at the further end of the garden, if this is where it will receive most sunshine.

Siting the patio

The patio is essentially an outdoor living area, a firm, dry level surface where you can relax in the sunshine or enjoy an alfresco meal. Although the most convenient place for a patio is close to the house, try and site it where it will receive maximum sunshine. This may mean a spot at the opposite end of the garden, in which case provide some form of permanent dry access from the house, such as a path or stepping stones. The size and shape of your patio can be an important element in the overall impact and success of your garden. If the traditional square or rectangle looks too formal or does little for a small, regular plot, experiment with curves and circles. Break up areas of hard landscaping with a change of level or integrated features, such as raised beds, a patio pool, built-in furniture or even a barbecue. Sometimes the choice of paving materials will influence the final shape and size of the area, so it makes sense to have some idea of how you want the patio to look before you make your final decision. If you can calculate the area using complete bricks, blocks or pavers, you will save yourself a lot of cutting and fitting at construction stage, as well as expensive wastage of materials.

Introducing a curve and a slight change of level is instantly softer and changes the whole look of the garden. Use your imagination at the early planning stages.

A free-standing patio makes an interesting option providing it can be well sheltered. Here, a circle is a good choice to liven up a regular square plot.

18

Positioning patios for the sun

Observe your garden during the course of the day to establish which areas are the sunniest at certain times. You could plan for two or even more patio areas, each serving a different purpose or designed to catch the best of the sun at different times of the day.

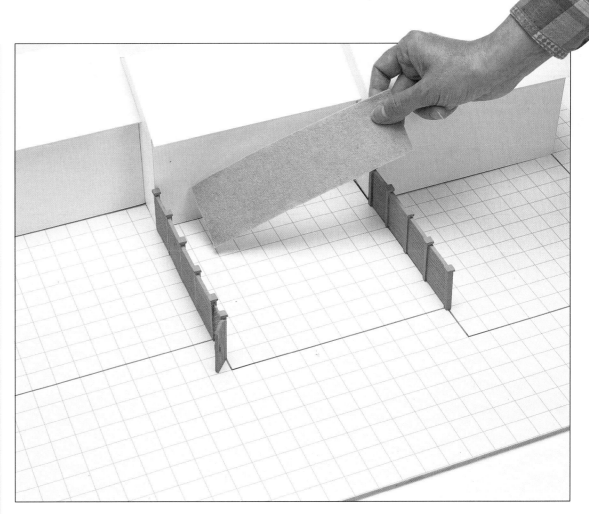

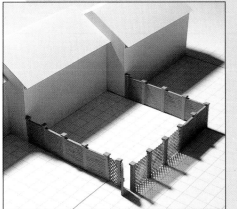

Left: Here, the house shades the area immediately beyond the back door for most of the day. This spot is unlikely to make a successful patio.

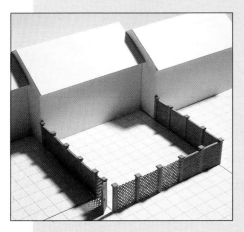

Left: An adjoining or nearby building may cast unwelcome shadows on certain parts of the garden.

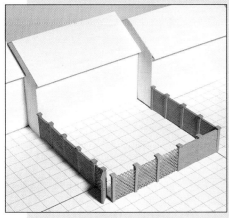

Left: In this situation, the whole garden is enjoying the benefits of full sunshine and only the front of the building is in shade.

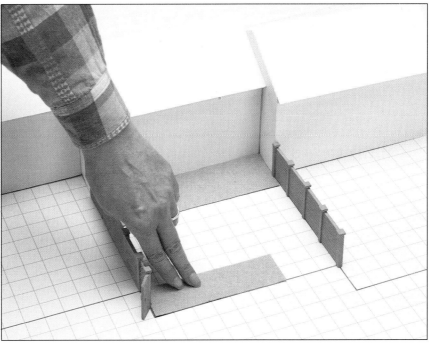

1 In the garden design shown above, the main patio is situated immediately behind the house, as this is the area that receives maximum sunshine right through the day.

2 A smaller paved seating area at the opposite end of the garden makes an excellent additional feature visually and is designed to catch the last rays of the afternoon sun.

A selection of patio styles

The most successful patio areas are planned as a complete concept in outdoor living. When you have decided on the facilities you want to include - seating, cooking (a barbecue), a hot tub for relaxation, an ornamental pool or built-in planting beds for scents and colors close at hand - you can choose the decorations and furnishings. It is usual to decide on the flooring first; will it be a configuration of paving slabs, a pattern of warm brick, friendly timber decking or a clever combination of different materials? The options, patterns and colors available mean that your design can be more creative than any floor indoors. Next, consider the 'walls'. Do you want living colors and textures with climbing plants smothering a trellis or pergola? Or do you prefer decorative screens and a background of evergreens? If your city backyard is stuck with an imposing high wall, paint it and hang it with plants on wall-mounted trellis. Patio furniture can be equally stylish: weather-resistant timber, simple but smart plastics or superbly upholstered seating for sunny days. Then there is the lighting - subtly concealed uplighters and downlighters fixed to walls or pergolas or hidden among the plants for evening enjoyment of your garden. Finish off with a few carefully chosen 'ornaments', such as coordinated tubs and pots for your patio plants, a statue, sundial or maybe a small moving water feature. Try to keep everything in style and the final effect will be stunning, especially if you take the trouble to color-coordinate even your plants and cushions, cloths and tableware.

Below: A private area behind a high wall with ornamental arches features a mass of sweet-scented climbers, such as roses and honeysuckle, and a cosy clutter of features and accessories.

Adding a decorative seat transforms any paved area into a private retreat.

Left: *This is truly an example of the patio as an outdoor living room. A smartly manicured patio in a well-tended garden has sophisticated upholstered furniture in soft pinks and whites that cleverly coordinates with the nearby blossom.*

Right: *The patio need not be large to offer a wide range of facilities. This secluded timber deck area includes a place to lounge and a hot tub for alfresco water fun.*

Below: *The patio is not always a secret or secluded feature. This open seating area is on full display to catch maximum sunshine and enjoy long views of the garden below.*

Different-sized paving slabs with contrasting brick edging have been arranged to create random patterns.

Below: *This is only one of several small patio areas around the garden, and is intended for all-year use, equipped as it is with durable, but attractive, wrought-iron furniture.*

Choosing the shape of your lawn

Grassy areas are not simply there to fill in the gaps between other features. A well-planned lawn can be an excellent design feature, even a focal point, if its shape and size is thoughtfully integrated into your general garden plan. Although a lawn requires a certain level of commitment in terms of maintenance, with trimming, watering, feeding and aerating during the growing season, grass is quick and easy to establish - whether from seed or turves - and can be adapted to any size or shape. However formal, it can offer a wonderfully soft, very natural effect that you could never achieve with an expanse of paving or hard landscaping and is complementary to all other features and materials. A lawn, especially where it has been planted in a definitive geometric shape such as a circle, rectangle or square, makes an excellent setting or surround for other features, such as a pond, a statue, flower beds or a sundial.

Above: A circular lawn immediately softens the hard-edged boundaries of a square plot and creates a more informal feel to the garden.

Above: Instead of positioning a square lawn dead center of a square site, try placing it on the diagonal, which produces a far more interesting effect.

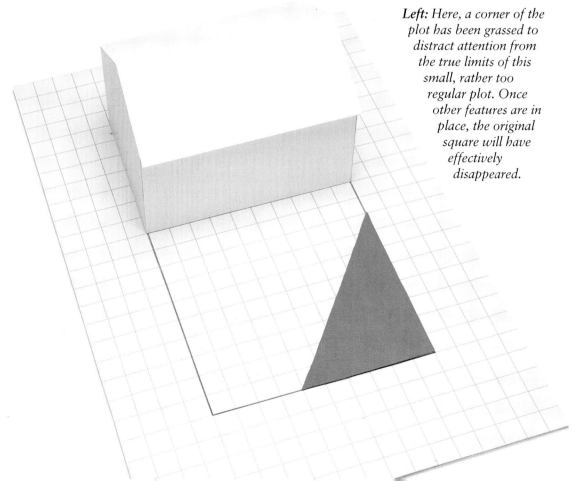

Left: Here, a corner of the plot has been grassed to distract attention from the true limits of this small, rather too regular plot. Once other features are in place, the original square will have effectively disappeared.

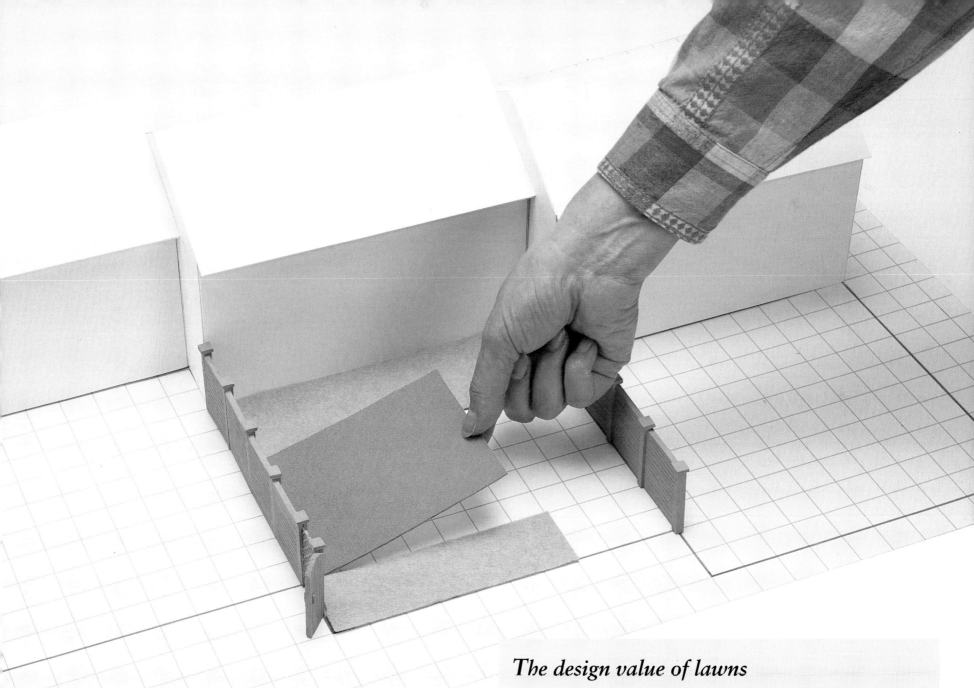

Above: *Here, a rectangular lawn forms part of the emerging design for this garden. Experiment with different shapes and sizes of lawn in conjunction with other features until you find something that looks good from every angle.*

The design value of lawns

You can use the lawn to link larger features, or to influence the visual impact of your garden as a whole. Its length, width, shape and position can make the plot appear wider, larger or simply more interesting than it actually is. Remember to plan an area of grass from a practical point of view, so that it is relatively easy to maintain. All parts must be accessible to your mower, with no areas narrower than the width of the machine. When experimenting with shapes, bear in mind that curves and circles create a softer, informal look, while harder, geometric figures, such as squares and rectangles, appear more formal. Try positioning your shapes on the diagonal or slightly at an angle for more interesting and less predictable effects.

Above: The green of a perfect lawn makes the most natural setting for beds and borders and can follow any informal shape, as long as you can mow it easily.

Below: In a very formal garden, grassy areas are usually restricted to sharply defined geometric shapes, so that the lawn forms a focal point on its own.

Featuring lawns in your garden design

There is no point in incorporating a lawn area into your garden design unless it is going to look good for at least most of the year, and good looks are as much due to good planning as they are to careful maintenance. Firstly, you should decide on what kind of grass area you need and the role it will play. A luxury lawn is not for hard wear areas that can so quickly develop bare or muddy patches. Small lawns can be a problem as they concentrate the wear. At least with a larger lawn you can rotate areas of hard wear, rather like you can with carpet tiles, to give them a chance to recover. Hard wear areas and gardens used by children and pets need a grass seed mixture with a high proportion of ryegrass, plus drought-resistant varieties, such as crested dog's tail, that will produce a good-quality, resilient turf that recovers quickly. Specialist grass seed suppliers can also make you up a mixture that contains clover in as high a percentage as you like. Although clover is completely unacceptable in a smart sward, it is hard-wearing, stays green during drought and can be mown like any lawn if you do not like the effect of the flowers. But for the classic velvet green stripes, you need a well-dug and raked, weed-free site and a special mixture of fine grasses, such as chewings fescue or browntop bent. These will guarantee that thick pile look, but you will have to play your part with controlling weeds, spiking, watering and, of course, mowing to the correct height with the right type of mower - one with a roller to make those stripes. Providing the weather is not too dry, you can cut a fine lawn shorter than a utility grass area; (0.5in)12mm in summer but 0.75in(20mm) in spring, summer and fall and during drought conditions. Water it regularly in dry weather to keep it looking green, but do not worry if it turns yellow during a drought - it will soon recover.

Above: *Edging the lawn in some decorative way, as with an attractive brick border, makes it easier to maintain and creates a more formal effect around beds and borders.*

Above: *Here, grass has been used to add fluidity and movement to an informal garden, as it flows like a wide green stream between trees and an interesting collection of foliage plants.*

Left: *This raised lawn area enclosed by a low clipped hedge is reminiscent of a castle keep and has produced an island of calm among a profusion of plants. An extensive, dense planting scheme emphasizes the relative order of this unexpected formal feature.*

Right: *A large circle of green velvet grass has been edged in brick and partially screened by a dense arrangement of plants to make a focal point of the small circular pool and fountain inset at the far end.*

Beds and borders

Plants are vital for softening the edges of your harder landscaping materials and for breathing life and color into your design. Plan for them at the earliest stages by incorporating suitable beds and borders into your main scheme. Left as an afterthought, beds and borders will not work nearly as well, because like other features, their shape and size can be crucial to the overall look of the garden or patio. Sometimes you will need to make provision for growing plants in conjunction with a particular feature, such as a spot to plant the climbers that are to smother a pergola. Beds with geometric shapes, perhaps raised and edged in matching materials, are an obvious choice for patio areas and might incorporate seating areas or even a pool, but they can work equally well as part of a more formal layout. The gentle curve of a less formal border is attractive and softens the effect of any garden, but do not make it too elaborate. Mark out the shape with a length of hosepipe when experimenting with an idea on site.

Right: The regular layout of a classic vegetable plot or formal herb garden means beds are easy to maintain, while presenting a certain well-ordered charm.

Left: Disguise the boundaries of a regular plot with informal plant borders. Be sure to make them unequal in size and length to achieve a more natural effect.

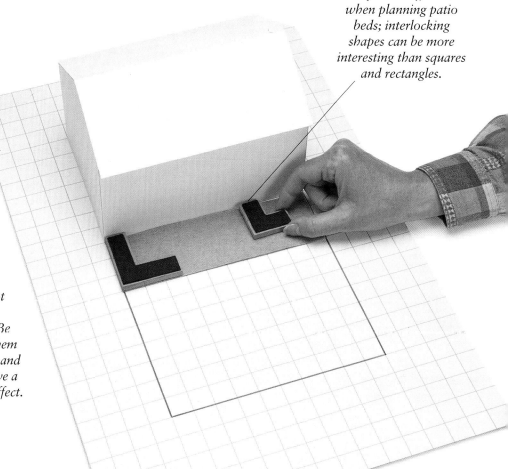

Use your imagination when planning patio beds; interlocking shapes can be more interesting than squares and rectangles.

2 *Raised beds incorporated into the patio design will successfully make the link between the paved area and the rest of the garden.*

1 *This island bed is positioned on the diagonal to create a diamond shape. It avoids the effect of a grassy formal border that a square cut out of the lawn would have created.*

Plants in borders

Consider the plants you will be incorporating into the beds, as this may influence their style and position. For example, bright annuals and scented plants are ideal for raised beds around the patio; herbs and vegetables need a good, sunny site; a pool, sculpture or seating area may require a backdrop of greenery.

Beds and borders to enhance your garden

Herbaceous borders and ornamental beds with annual color can be very time-consuming unless you plan them carefully. First ensure that all parts of the bed or border are easily accessible by not making them too wide or too deep. Then, reduce the amount of weeding and watering by using dense ground cover plants or mulch with bark chips or even black plastic between the plants, at least until they have become established. Covering every bit of soil with leaves or flowers looks more attractive and smothers unwelcome weeds, as well as reducing moisture loss. Your choice of plants will also affect the amount of time you spend on routine maintenance. Design a good backbone of evergreens, shrubs and reliable perennials and you will reduce grubbing out and replanting through the months. Use a few annuals only for seasonal color and interest in selected areas, depending on how much time and inclination you have for sowing and transplanting. You might also be selective with the varieties you choose; some of the newer types have been deliberately bred so that they are shorter than traditional ones, so that you can still grow your favorites without the need for staking. Also look out for plants that are recommended as free-flowering, which means that they keep on producing blooms for several months. If you are planning raised beds, you will save time and trouble later on if you incorporate a good drainage system at the construction stage. You might leave occasional gaps in the brick joints or insert small pipes designed to drain into a suitable gulley. You may also consider a built-in automatic watering system to prevent the soil drying out in warmer weather.

Above: This sweeping border echoes the profile of the path and lawn. An ordered planting scheme emphasizes the effect, with begonias flowing down from a bed of dahlias.

Right: Conifers add height and winter interest to your island beds. Aim for a good variety of heights, shapes and colors to complement the bright annual planting in the foreground.

Right: *Herbs are perfect for creating a formal patchwork effect of subtle colors and textures. Divide a square or circular bed into even sections and plant a different herb in each part. To maintain the effect, you will need to trim back some of the more rampant species from time to time.*

Variegated lemon balm (Melissa) contributes a light touch and soft feltlike leaf textures.

Below: *In a cottage-style garden, a profusion of many different plants is allowed to create an informal mass of shapes and colors that conceals what is essentially a formal arrangement of paths and planting beds.*

Tiny-leaved thyme (Thymus) is available in many forms and colors and is ideal for creating 'carpet' effects.

Below: *These tight rows of edible plants edged with curly green parsley have been chosen for their decorative, as well as practical value, with 'Lollo rosso' lettuce and pretty strawberries.*

Planning a pool

The light-reflecting properties of water in a pond or pool in the garden or on a patio immediately add a new dimension to your design. A pool is a natural focal point and makes a stunning, easy-care feature once installed. It also gives you the opportunity to grow a selection of exciting water plants or to install a moving water feature, such as a fountain, spout or cascade, to add sound and sparkle to the scheme. Position a pool carefully within the plot and consider the practical implications, as well as the design possibilities. Water and water plants need plenty of light and sunshine, so avoid a shady spot. Try not to position a pool too near to trees, as falling leaves can pollute the water, or too close to a boundary, where you might have construction and maintenance problems. For an informal, natural pool sketch out a rough kidney shape without too many inlets as these are difficult to construct. Alternatively, choose a more formal square, rectangle or circle, which could be raised or sunk into the ground. You might even consider two or more pools linked by a water spout or cascade to produce an interesting change of level on the patio or to link patio to garden.

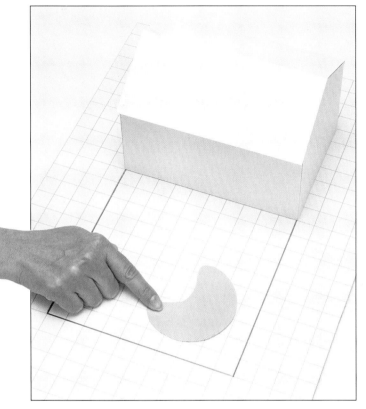

Left: An informal kidney shape makes an excellent starting point for a natural pond or pool.

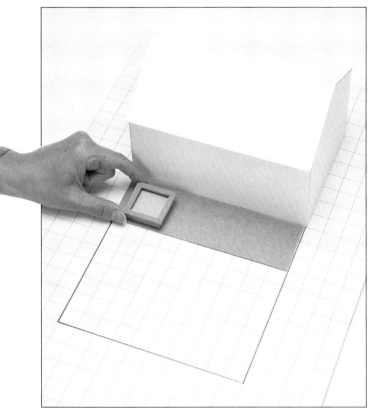

Left: A patio pool can be designed to fit the shape and size of an existing paved area, and raised up if excavation work is not practical.

Left: Here, a round pool takes its lead from a circular grassed area and transforms the lawn into an important focal point.

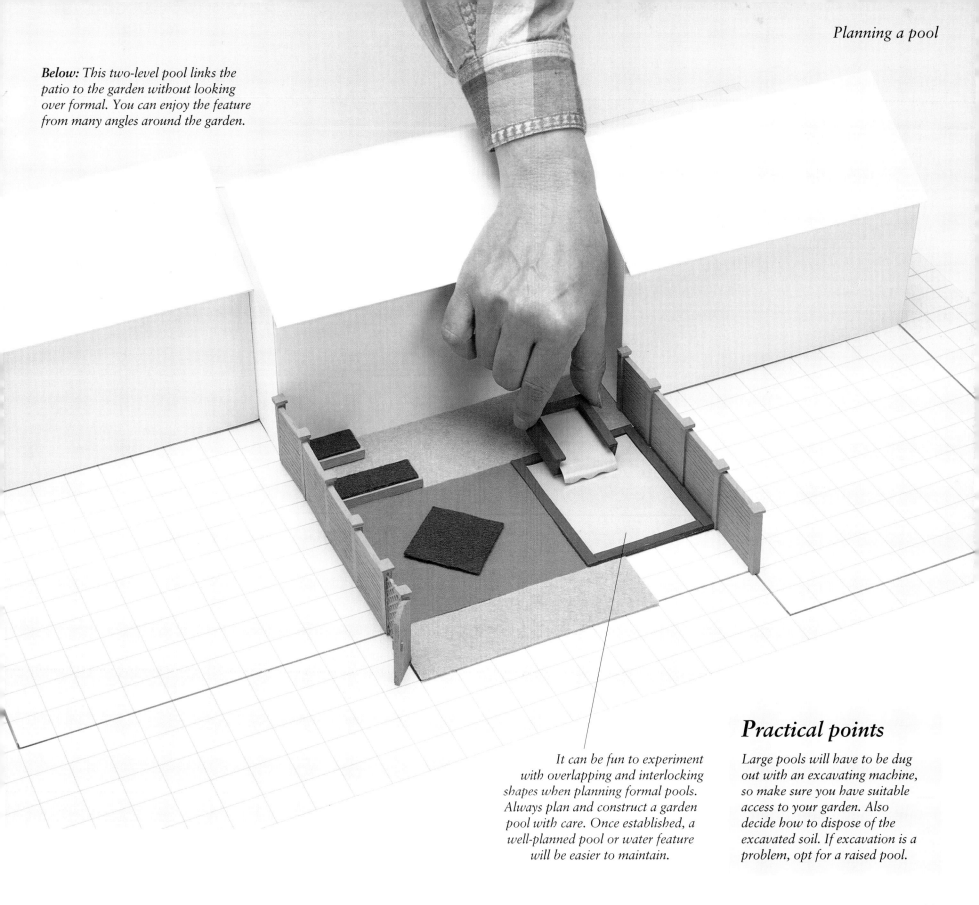

Below: *This two-level pool links the patio to the garden without looking over formal. You can enjoy the feature from many angles around the garden.*

It can be fun to experiment with overlapping and interlocking shapes when planning formal pools. Always plan and construct a garden pool with care. Once established, a well-planned pool or water feature will be easier to maintain.

Practical points

Large pools will have to be dug out with an excavating machine, so make sure you have suitable access to your garden. Also decide how to dispose of the excavated soil. If excavation is a problem, opt for a raised pool.

Water in the garden

As well as shape and style, the materials you choose to edge your pool will significantly influence its final look and suitability to your garden. Formal pools tend to be edged in brick, stone or paving to match other features in the garden. Grass, pebbles and other natural materials combined with suitable pool-edge plants are more in keeping with informal ponds. Adding a moving water feature, such as a fountain, waterspout, cascade or waterfall, to suit the style of your pond will introduce delightful sounds and a sparkle to the water. The kind of plants you can grow in the damp conditions in and around a pool or pond are quite unlike any others in the garden. They are lush and glossy, often dramatic, and a well-planned display can include a marvellous variety of shapes and forms. Each plant group is suited to a particular environment and will thrive with very little care, providing it is in the right place. In the water itself, you can plant beautiful water lilies in open mesh containers of rich aquatic potting mixture. They spread rapidly, so do not grow many varieties, even in large pools. There are many beautiful forms and sizes to choose from.

Above: An interesting planting scheme includes a good variety of color and shape to provide an excellent backdrop and fine reflections around this informal pool.

An ornamental fountain makes a special feature of the smallest pool.

Left: A small formal pond can make a focal point in an informal garden, too. This brick-edged circular pool is partially hidden by shrubs and hostas.

Above: In this formal complex, the limited planting helps the pool to retain its sharp outline edged in brick and glossy blue-stained timber seating.

A circular pool can be formal without looking hard-edged, and makes an attractive raised feature, complete with fountain.

A formal square is ideal for pools on different levels and with interlocking effects.

An informal lagoon shape offers plenty of scope for a large pool and can follow the contours of the site. Do not make it too complicated; the narrow areas here will restrict water flow and cause stagnation.

A rectangle is a popular choice for large formal pools on the patio and in the garden, and can include a wide range of features.

A simple kidney shape is perfect for most informal settings. It is often semi-concealed beneath a display of moisture-loving plants.

Right: *Dense planting recreates the effect of a natural stream, with a good variety of marginal and moisture-loving plants along the banks, and hostas and mosses in the foreground.*

Right: *This formal, brick-edged pool has a suitable backdrop of shrubs and an ornamental wall complete with a sunburst water spout. Plants in pots are used to soften the foreground.*

Below: *Small water features add something of interest in the smallest corner of the garden or patio.*

Paths and walkways

An essential item in the garden is some form of access that remains reasonably dry and safe underfoot in all weathers and allows you to move from one feature to another. Without it, you will create unsightly tracks and the garden will become a swamp in winter. But walkways, paths and stepping stones have important design possibilities, too. They can look strictly formal, carving the plot into distinct geometric shapes, or they can meander between features creating a more relaxed feel. Because the eye naturally follows the shape and line of any pathway into the distance and beyond, the path can influence the appearance and shape of the site visually. Take it straight from A to B and the plot seems shorter, but describe a more circuitous route and the garden instantly appears bigger and more interesting, especially if you cannot see right to the end. If a solid path seems too dominant, use the broken effect of stepping stones or a staggered timber walkway. The materials you use will influence the look and feel of your garden; concrete is practical and suits the vegetable plot; stone slabs and pavers can be adapted to both formal and informal schemes. For a country cottage style, lay brick in ornamental herringbone and basketweave patterns, or for a woodland feel, lay down a path of wood chips with log slices as stepping stones.

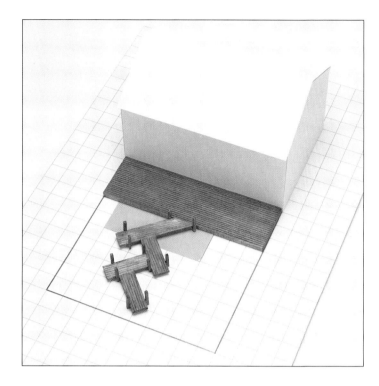

Above: A staggered timber walkway running from a patio or timber-decked area is stylish and simple to install. It is also a clever way to deal with the problem of a sloping garden.

Left: A strict framework of concrete or paving slab paths will immediately divide your garden into a formal arrangement of planting beds that may appear uncompromising but has a pleasing symmetry.

Left: A less formal route, created using stepping stones, can make the same size and shape plot look and feel completely different. This type of path cleverly distracts the eye away from the true, straight boundaries of the garden.

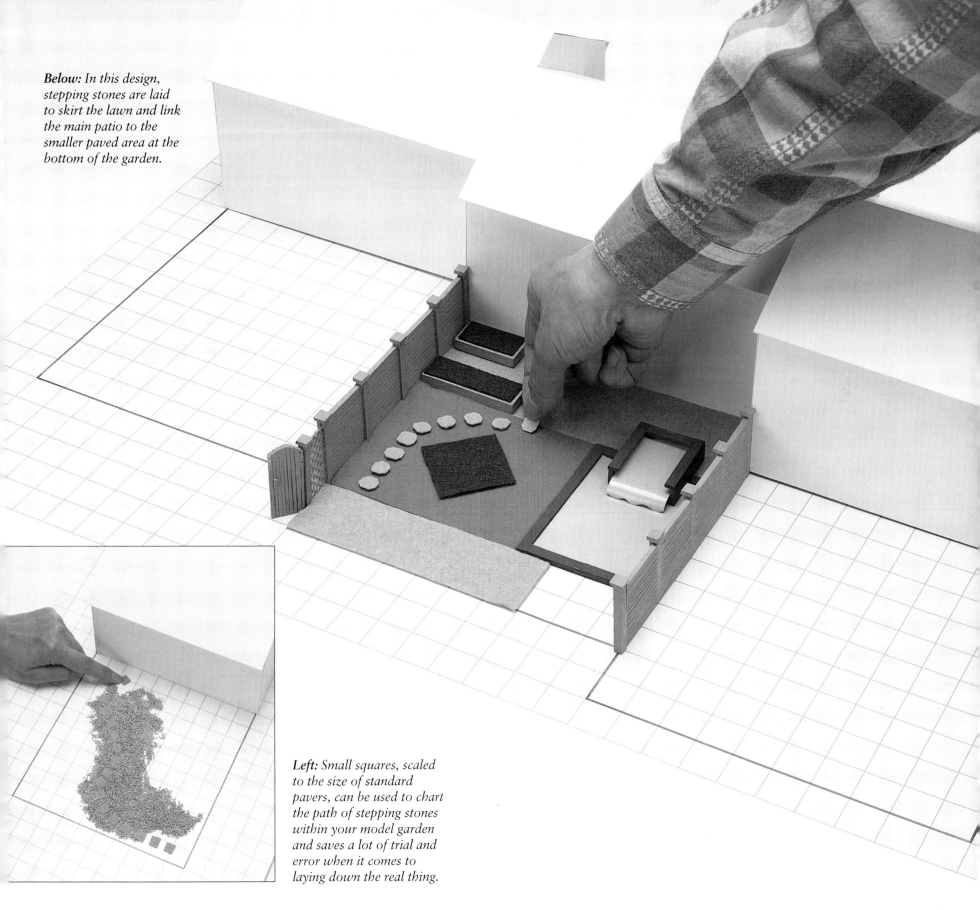

Below: In this design, stepping stones are laid to skirt the lawn and link the main patio to the smaller paved area at the bottom of the garden.

Left: Small squares, scaled to the size of standard pavers, can be used to chart the path of stepping stones within your model garden and saves a lot of trial and error when it comes to laying down the real thing.

A walk through the garden

Like other hard landscaping features, paths and walkways improve if their shape and structure are visually softened or even partially obscured. It makes them less dominant and encourages them to blend into the general garden scheme. Stepping stones have a naturally broken effect, but even they can be softened by letting the surrounding grass or chippings cover the edges of each slab. A path along a planting bed or border will probably have plants spilling over the edge; low-growing, carpet-forming varieties at the front of your planting scheme are easier to control. Tiny prostrate plants, such as creeping thyme, are also useful for growing between the pavers or bricks of a path, and produce a mature and colorful effect. In a formal scheme, you could strategically position tubs or pots of plants along the route for a more controlled look, or use urns or an elegant piece of sculpture for a more architectural feel. Plants in containers are a useful way to soften the edges and corners of a raised timbered walkway. Alternatively, plant clumps of various tall species in the corners created by a zigzag configuration to add height and interest.

Above: Hexagonal pavers make a strong pattern of stepping stones across the lawn. Keep the grass trimmed to retain their clear outline.

Above: A change of level and variety of materials in this formal path and steps add interest around a carefully planted site. Plants soften the edges and make the path less dominant.

Left: A flagstone path always has a lovely mellow appearance, especially when set in gravel and softened by plants and boulders. Lay the flags in random patterns for the best effect.

Left: *Slightly raised, timber-decked paths and walkways are quick and easy to install. Here, the walkway is more like a bridge, partially submerged in a sea of attractive perennials, including* Astilbe, Lamium, Alchemilla *and* Astrantia.

Scour the timber surface periodically with a wire brush to remove slippery moss and algae growth.

Below: *A gravel path suits formal and informal gardens alike. The edges might be contained by stone kerbings or timber battens. Here, they have been allowed to disappear beneath a sprawl of summer plants, such as* Heuchera, *fennel and geranium.*

Below: *Crazy paving or gravel always produces a natural, informal effect, yet is smart enough to be incorporated into a more formal scheme. Here the edges are softened by hostas.*

Trellis and screening

Trellis and screens might be considered rather functional pieces of garden apparatus - they shelter, they hide, they provide support for climbing plants. But they can work magic, too: clever illusions that will transform gardens both large and small into places of interest and intrigue. Use them to disguise features you would rather not see, such as an ugly fence, the shed or utility area, or to divide the plot into more interesting, secluded areas or 'garden rooms'. These might have a special theme, such as an oriental garden, a single color scheme, a place for meditation or an area of particular seasonal interest, such as a winter garden. If you are going to smother the structure in plants, something basic, such as diamond trellis panels, should be fine, providing you select a type strong enough to take the weight of your proposed plants. Along a boundary, for weighty climbers, or where the trellis might have to withstand strong winds, go for the stronger panels, which are often the same size and strength as fence panels, and erect them in the same way as you would a fence. You can buy a wide range of ornamental styles from gothic to oriental, in different finishes, such as natural stain or colored varnishes.

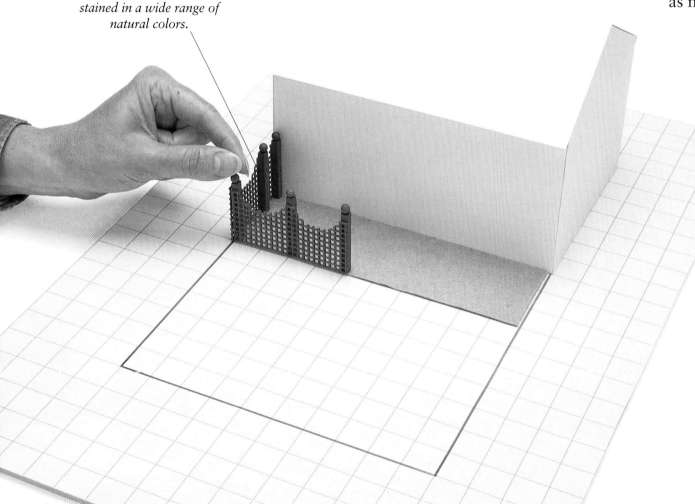

Above: Simple plant supports can be used to add height and interest anywhere in the garden. These wired posts are ideal for cordon fruit trees.

Trellis can be painted or stained in a wide range of natural colors.

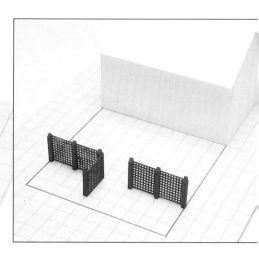

Above: Use standard sections of trellis to divide the garden into more interesting areas, each with its own theme or particular atmosphere.

Left: Sturdy or ornamental trellis might shelter a patio from unpleasant drafts or create a private area where you can relax in seclusion.

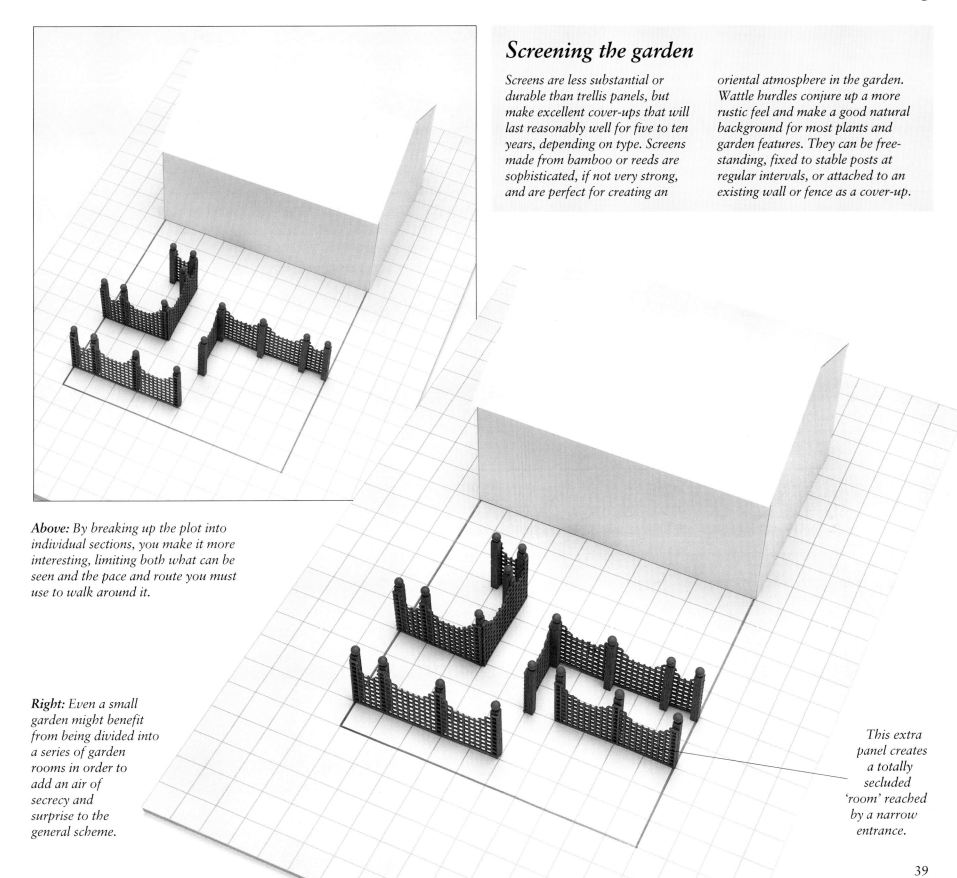

Screening the garden

Screens are less substantial or durable than trellis panels, but make excellent cover-ups that will last reasonably well for five to ten years, depending on type. Screens made from bamboo or reeds are sophisticated, if not very strong, and are perfect for creating an oriental atmosphere in the garden. Wattle hurdles conjure up a more rustic feel and make a good natural background for most plants and garden features. They can be free-standing, fixed to stable posts at regular intervals, or attached to an existing wall or fence as a cover-up.

Above: By breaking up the plot into individual sections, you make it more interesting, limiting both what can be seen and the pace and route you must use to walk around it.

Right: Even a small garden might benefit from being divided into a series of garden rooms in order to add an air of secrecy and surprise to the general scheme.

This extra panel creates a totally secluded 'room' reached by a narrow entrance.

Planting up trellis and screens

Most styles of trellis and screen are attractive and some are highly decorative, yet all will benefit from the softening effect of at least one climbing or creeping plant to add life, color and seasonal interest. That said, you must choose your plants carefully. A weighty plant would soon drag over a lightweight framework; others, such as the fast-growing Russian vine or wisteria, which has thick stems that can damage roof tiles or down pipes on adjoining buildings, might prove too invasive. Plants climb and attach themselves to supports in various ways. Some need a little help or training; twining plants, for example, soon look untidy if not kept in check. Others, such as ivy, and the climbing hydrangea, cling to the support by means of small roots along the stems and need little assistance. When fixing a trellis against a wall or fence, it is a good idea to keep a space between them using vertical wooden lathes so that the plant can twine itself right round the support and you can also lift it away for maintenance. Of course, you can train climbing and twining plants using only minimum support, such as a series of taut wires, a wigwam of poles or even a line or posts strung with ropes. For a permanent leafy effect, consider hedging plants as a form of screening within the garden. Once established, a hedge is long-lived and produces a lovely natural effect.

Right: Plant-covered trellis has been used in this garden as a divider, which helps to restrict your view of the site as a whole, and consequently makes it appear more interesting.

Above: In a small garden you can use trellis to create optical illusions like this arrangement of blue-stained trellis and matching evergreens to produce a telescope effect among the greenery.

Below: By painting the trellis white, a newly secluded area gains an impression of lightness. Pastel-shaded paving slabs and white flowers reinforce the relaxing effect.

Left: *An elaborate trellis construction is a major feature of this garden. It has been used to separate different parts of the plot and create more secluded but stylish areas.*

Below: *This simple wooden trellis strikes exactly the right balance between a more formal part of the garden and a woodland area beyond. Climbing plants help to soften the link.*

On a trellis, a quick-flowering annual, such as this Ipomoea purpurea (morning glory), creates a temporary effect while you are waiting for perennial climbers to mature.

Below: *An ugly or boring high wall is easily disguised using sections of trellis. Here climbing plants are already being trained up the structure.*

Black paint adds a dramatic touch to trellis.

Arches and pergolas

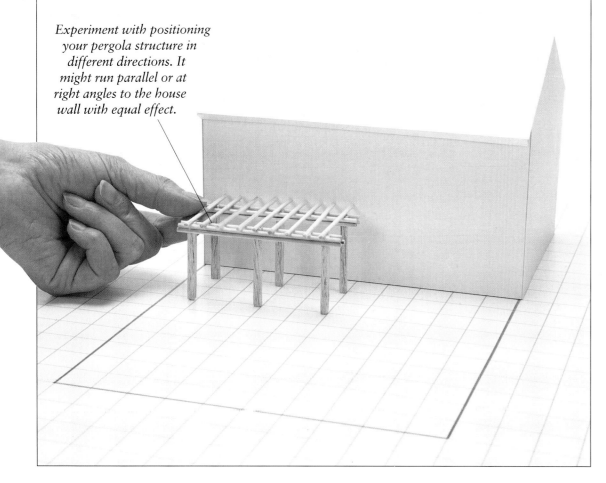

Above: *A series of arches makes a delightful feature and a wonderful flowery walk when the framework is covered in a profusion of plants.*

Experiment with positioning your pergola structure in different directions. It might run parallel or at right angles to the house wall with equal effect.

An archway or pergola not only provides a useful support for attractive climbing plants, but also adds height and a new dimension to the garden or patio by creating an ornamental entrance or walkway. This naturally encourages you to pass through it and also frames the area of garden beyond. Archways come in many guises, from rustic-style poles clothed in sweet-scented roses or honeysuckle to more formal timber shapes or ornamental, wrought metal. A series of simple metal hoops can be most effective bordering a patio or part of the garden once it is festooned with leaves and flowers. A pergola serves a dual purpose: it might be used as a walkway to lead from one part of the garden to another or to show off a particular group of climbing plants, such as a wisteria walk. It can be erected as an attractive form of shelter or shade over the patio or similar seating area, using a selection of leafy climbing plants or pull-over bamboo screens to protect you from strong sunshine and light summer showers. Again, the materials used in construction will dictate the look of the feature and affect the whole atmosphere of the patio or garden. You can use larch or chestnut poles for a rustic feel or sawn timber for a more formal scheme, maybe in conjunction with brick pillars to match nearby hard-landscaped features. If the site is a windy one, you could infill the sides with bamboo screens, lattice fencing or even vertical or diagonally arranged boarding to keep out the worst of any drafts.

Left: *A pergola might adjoin a building or be totally free-standing in order to shade a paved or patio area. Plants or screens will protect diners from strong sunshine or light showers.*

Above: *As part of the main garden design, an ornamental timber archway makes a decorative entrance to the small paved area at the end of the plot and frames a view.*

Framing the view or a leafy shelter

A tall, dominant feature, such as an arch or pergola, must have some functional relevance, as well as a decorative purpose. Like a bridge or path, it is a nonsense unless it really does lead somewhere, or at least, in the case of a pergola, shades a patio or paved area. Ideally, link the feature to a related structure: a timber archway making a break in a fence, or an ornamental brick or wrought-iron arch adding interest to a high wall. A pergola might link house to garden, or be positioned over an existing path to create a covered walkway. It looks more in keeping if you can use the right style and materials. Match brick to brick, use the same stained timber that you chose for fencing or a trellis, or build an arch or pergola with rustic poles to suit a country-style scheme. Remember to consider the height and width of your feature. If you are using an arch to frame a view, site it in exactly the right place to make that view a good one. Check that people can walk through it without stooping, remembering that later it will be festooned with climbing plants. Width can be crucial, too, especially if you need to take a lawn mower or wheelbarrow through. A pergola need not cover the whole patio, but make sure that it shades the seating area comfortably and that the pillars do not spoil your view or cause an obstruction. It is attention to detail that makes a good design successful.

Climbing plants trained overhead provide shade and shelter through this walkway.

Left: A large stone urn on a matching pedestal makes a splendid focal point at the end of an ornamental archway smothered in vigorous creepers.

Left: *This large, simply built, timber pergola creates a covered walkway hung with 'Rambling Rector' roses. Lush planting at the base softens the effect of the supporting pillars.*

Right: *A combination of materials can create a more elaborate pergola structure. Here, brick pillars and wooden poles, almost hidden under climbing roses, frame and soften a geometric layout of paths and paving.*

Below: *An arch can be used to frame a view, as well as to make an entrance. This classical statue in its green leafy arbor takes on a magical quality when viewed through a rustic archway.*

Clematis montana is a useful quick-growing climber that provides attractive cover and a mass of pink or white blooms.

Right: *This pergola has been used to add height and interest to the garden by shading a curving path, thus allowing it to wind intriguingly out of sight.*

Positioning trees

Trees are essential to your background planting scheme, providing height and a sense of maturity even to the most modest garden. If you do not have the space or the time to wait for a proper leafy backdrop, you could always plant a small single specimen tree in a strategic position - preferably one that can offer spectacular spring blossom, fine summer foliage, glorious fall color and interesting winter fruits all in the one species. Alternatively, miniaturize the look in a formal garden with a pair of clipped evergreens in pots on either side of steps or an ornamental seat. Even dwarf conifers have their place, providing height and winter interest in containers around the patio or in the rockery. Larger gardens can enjoy larger-scale effects, such as a leafy screen or backdrop to provide total seclusion, a shady bower or an elegant avenue. When planning trees, always allow for the true spread and height of each species, so that it will neither be cramped by other features nor likely to create a nuisance or hazard to nearby buildings or a pond. A wall-trained tree should not be planted any closer to the wall than 12in(30cm) to ensure stability and soil fertility. Some areas will prove unsuitable for planting trees because of an existing drainage system or too shallow a soil with a layer of impenetrable rock below. Here, growing the trees in raised beds or containers may be the answer.

Above: Do not plant a tree any closer to a building than its ultimate spread. Cutting branches will spoil its shape and produce a lopsided effect.

Below: At the rear of the garden, trees do not interfere with anything else and make a fine view or a leafy backdrop for other garden features.

Below: Where you are planning a group of trees, odd numbers often create a better effect than even ones. Try for a range of heights and canopy shapes within the group.

Above: *Do not site trees close to a pool or pond, where shade and falling leaves can be a problem, causing green scum and pollution in the water.*

Above: *Keeping water features clear of the tree's shadow will save you time and trouble, as plants and water need light if they are to function properly.*

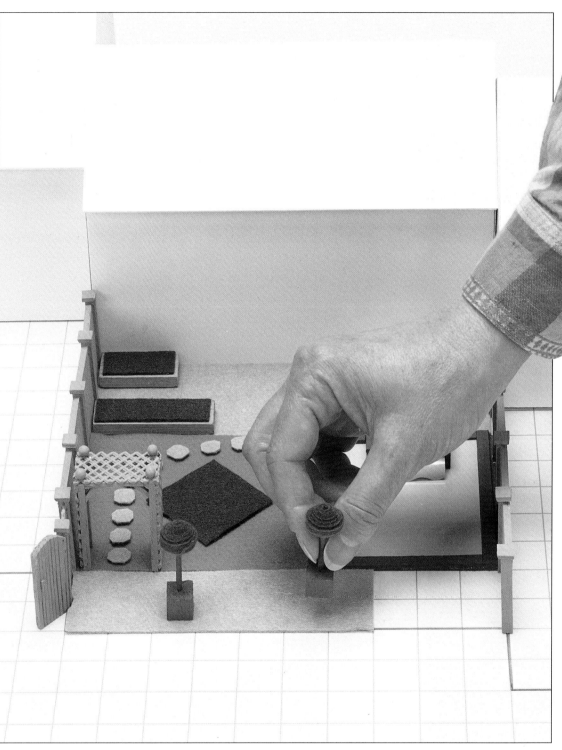

Above: *In this small, semi-formal garden, with large areas given over to water and paving for easy maintenance, the choice of trees has been restricted to a pair of clipped bay trees in decorative tubs. These add height and style to the small paved seating area at the end of the garden.*

47

Using trees in the garden

Trees may be useful large and complex features within the garden or larger landscape, but standing alone in a bare patch of earth, they will only look disjointed and out of place. Even a single specimen tree needs to relate to surrounding plants and be underplanted with some kind of complementary colors or seasonal interest for times when the tree is not looking its best. Proper consideration given to the areas around and beneath your trees will certainly ensure that they blend well into the rest of your garden scheme. Shrubs are a logical progression downwards, but not all are compatible with certain trees. Large shrubs, such as rhododendron, will not thrive near shallow-rooted trees such as birch and ash, for example. On a bank or steep slope, a scrambling plant, such as the glossy evergreen bramble, *Rubus tricolor*, will help to bind and stabilize the soil. At ground level directly beneath the tree conditions will dictate what plants you might grow successfully. Under trees with a dense canopy of foliage, such as the horse chestnut, the rain cannot penetrate and the soil is too dry for most plants. Here, an area of pebbles or bark chips may be the best option. Elsewhere, look for quick-growing, creeping and ground cover plants that thrive in dappled shade. For moist areas, woodland species, such as the spotted lungwort, *Pulmonaria*, or sweet-scented lily of the valley make a welcome sight. Dry shade can be more difficult to choose plants for, but drought-loving grasses, such as the Japanese mondo grass or dwarf bamboos, will make good growth and create a fine display. In spring, the area below trees is perfect for a bright show of spring bulbs among the grass, including snowdrops, narcissi and aconites.

Above: The base of this pretty Cercis chinensis *grown as a specimen tree has been planted with* Colchicum speciosum *'Album' to provide special seasonal interest at ground level.*

Right: This area of the garden comes alive in spring with a mass of pink, red and white tulips in the long grass beneath the pink and white petals of cherry and pear blossom.

When planting bulbs, aim to create a massed effect, not small clumps of a few flowers.

Left: Soon this laburnum walk will be a blaze of glorious yellow blooms, but for now, tulips planted below provide a little early season interest.

Right: The different shapes and colors of conifers create some unusual and striking all-season effects. Here, Juniperus communis compressa and 'Blue Haze' rise out of a sea of Abies procera 'Glauca prostrata'.

Below: Buddleia alternifolia can be trained to create a weeping tree covered in scented clusters of pink blossoms in early summer. It makes a spectacular highlight in the shrubbery.

Planning a rockery

You may have an interesting slope or hummock to plant up, or perhaps you want to introduce a little height and variety, and use up a mound of excavated soil from building a patio or pool. A rock or alpine garden is a natural and highly attractive option, but make sure that the proposed site is away from the shade and invasive roots of any nearby trees and that it is well drained, with access to plenty of light and sunshine. The ideal site should slope gently in the direction in which the sun shines at midday, with shelter from prevailing winds. In a small garden, perfection may not be possible, but do try to avoid drafty or shady areas. The feature should look in keeping with its surroundings, so do not make it too steep and view it from every angle to check that it blends in with adjoining features. A rockery always looks particularly good as the backdrop to an informal pool, especially if you incorporate a small waterfall into the feature.

Above: A rockery, complete with a waterfall using a pump and concealed liner, makes the perfect natural backdrop behind an informal pool.

Small rockeries

If the site just does not have the space or potential for a rockery, then create a smaller alpine feature, such as a paved or gravel scree garden, with suitable plants between the slabs or pebbles; or convert an old porcelain sink into a miniature rock garden by disguising it with hypertufa - a mixture of equal parts by volume of cement, gritty sand and peat, which sets like stone. With a good layer of rubble for drainage (about 3in/7.5cm), and a free-draining, sandy potting mix, a few boulders and gravel mulch, it will be the perfect setting for a few of your favorite alpines.

Left: A larger alpine feature can add height and an interesting change of level to an otherwise dull site, and offers the chance to display a wide selection of attractive plants.

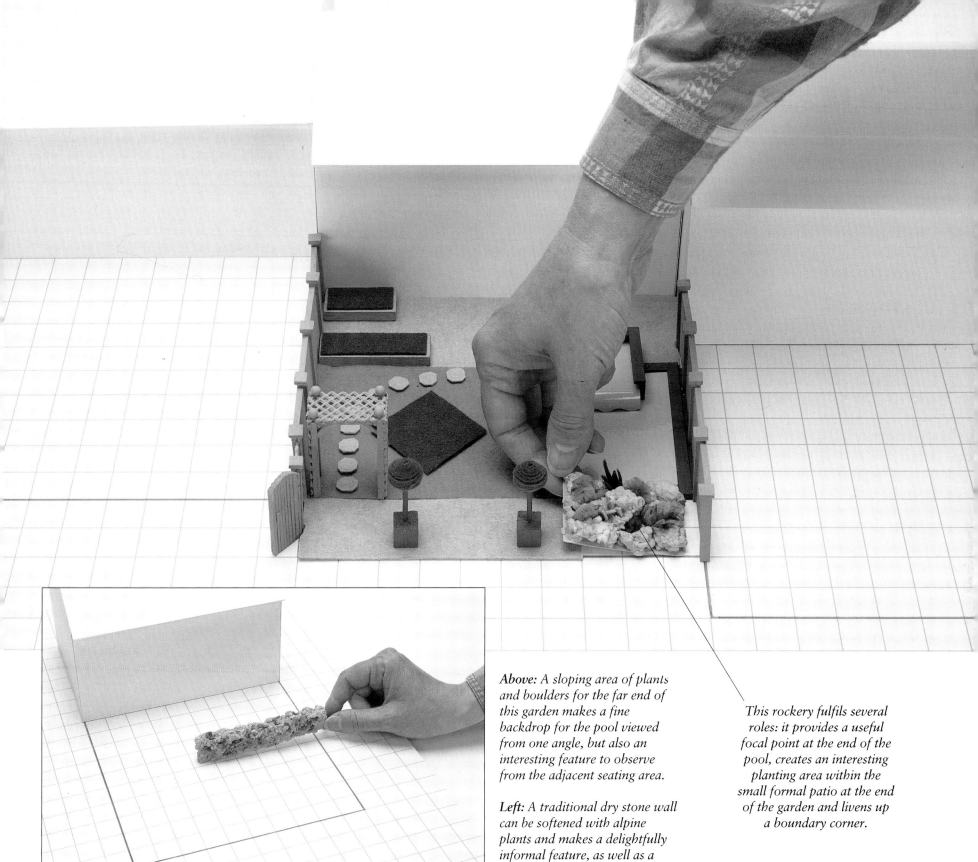

Above: A sloping area of plants and boulders for the far end of this garden makes a fine backdrop for the pool viewed from one angle, but also an interesting feature to observe from the adjacent seating area.

Left: A traditional dry stone wall can be softened with alpine plants and makes a delightfully informal feature, as well as a means of dividing the garden.

This rockery fulfils several roles: it provides a useful focal point at the end of the pool, creates an interesting planting area within the small formal patio at the end of the garden and livens up a boundary corner.

Rockery features

The rock or stone in your rockery is as important as the plants themselves. Local stone will look more in keeping and may be cheaper to transport, but whatever you choose, keep to one sort of stone for a natural effect. Limestone is popular for rock gardens as it looks natural and absorbs moisture, which encourages alpine plants to cling to its surface. Sandstone is relatively lightweight and very attractive, but prone to frost damage. Natural tufa is full of tiny holes, ideal for small plants, but expensive to use on a large scale. Rocks should retain soil and keep plant roots moist and cool, so bury them firmly, with at least one third of their bulk in the ground, and pack the soil tightly around them. Ensure that the strata of each boulder or rock is on the same plane and tilt the rocks slightly backwards to allow water to run towards the plants. Do not cover the whole rockery with rock; leave plenty of large areas free for growing plants. Position the rocks or stones close to each other in groups, with little more than a crevice between them. Pack this with soil, making sure there are no air pockets, and insert a plant. Do not scatter the rocks randomly, as this never looks natural.

Left: Vertical gardening at its most natural: an old stone wall virtually hidden by flowers and foliage. Suitable plants can be inserted into crevices between the stones.

Above: A sunny sheltered site with good drainage is ideal for alpines. The soil between them is well mulched to reduce moisture loss while the plants are maturing to fill the gaps.

Left: *A rock garden and pool feature work well together. Here, tiny plants have been tucked into pockets of soil between the rocks, while iris and dwarf conifers add height and a miniature landscape effect among saxifrages, primulas and Aquilegia trifolium.*

Below: *This is the rock garden tamed and transferred to a formal setting. A clever arrangement within a raised bed has been linked to a small pool in a barrel to create a compact yet complex multi-faceted feature.*

Left: *A rockery can form an integral part of a permanent border. This dry sunny area has been studded with stones and planted with alpines to add interest among lusher perennial plants.*

Finishing touches

With the plan finished and all the major hard landscaping features in place, you now have a good idea of how your garden is going to look and work. What comes next will be the ornaments, plants and flowers that add color, texture and interest to your scheme. You can see how the model garden has taken shape; even without plants and finishing touches, the garden has been transformed. Clever shapes and the siting of major features distract from the boundaries and create several alternative focal points around the garden: an extensive pool area, a well-equipped patio close to the house, a small lawn and a further seating area at the opposite end of the plot. Now it needs something to soften those hard edges and add some individuality and interest. Decorative pots, tubs and other ornamental containers are invaluable for positioning plants around the patio and other paved areas, and can be used to great effect to soften steps, paths or pool surrounds. A sundial, sculpture or birdbath adds interest to a dull corner or creates a focal point on the patio or in the center of the lawn.

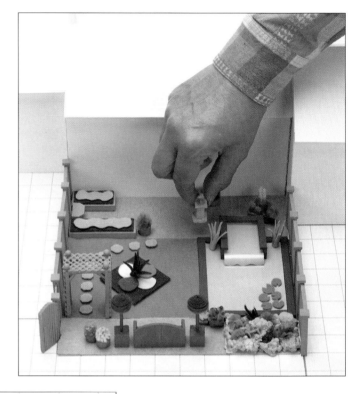

Above: Adding the finishing touches can be fun. Try to keep the style of containers, ornaments and furniture in keeping with the general theme or atmosphere you have tried to create.

Left: The finished plan can be assessed to see if the features fit together well and whether they work on a practical level. Now is the time to change any details you are not happy with before the real construction work begins.

Remember that you can buy ornaments and decorative accessories that have been specially adapted for pools and water features.

Right: The garden that started life as a dull and rather limited square plot is going to be smart and stylish, with a wide range of easy-to-maintain features in a surprisingly small area.

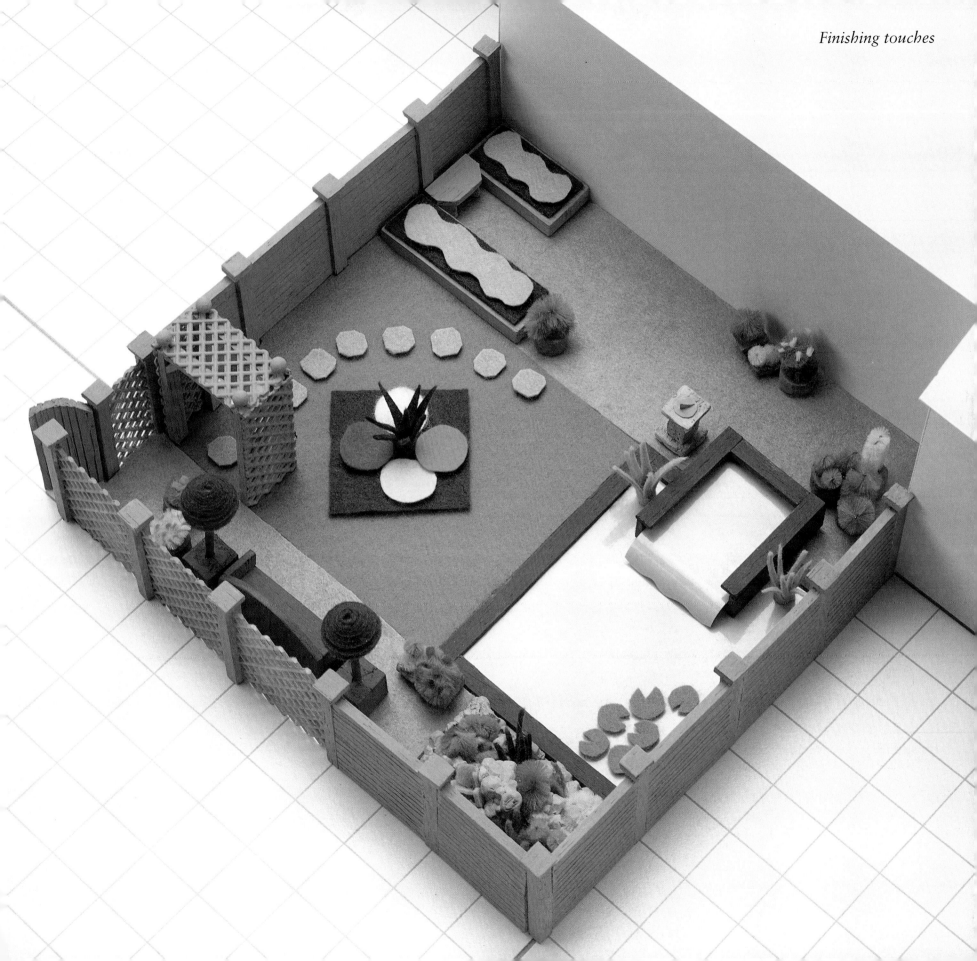

Making your garden special

Garden ornaments and accessories can be used to reinforce a theme or to create one. Even a careful choice of containers can conjure up a certain atmosphere: terracotta for a Mediterranean feel, old wooden barrels for a rustic look, painted Versailles planters or traditional stone urns to decorate a formal scheme. Add to these the appropriate outdoor furniture and accessories and, later, a suitable selection of plants, and the setting is complete. Garden furniture is available in an equally wide range of styles, from rustic wooden benches as resting places anywhere around the garden, to decorative Lutyens-inspired seats for positioning in arbors or at the end of a vista. Dining sets and furniture for relaxing on the patio might be easy-care, attractive plastic, smart all-season timber or old-fashioned, fancy wrought-iron. The opportunities and the looks you can create are endless, but make sure yours are in tune with the rest of your garden design. Positioning these final features is equally important.

Plant containers tend to look best arranged in odd numbers, such as threes or fives. Use different sizes and heights to good effect, but the same or a similar finish is important if they are to look good together. For a more formal look, position tubs or pots geometrically - on either side of an entrance or flanking a seat. Small ornaments can be added for variety; or give them more importance by raising them up to eye level on a platform or plinth to create a focal point on the patio or lawn.

The small pots are raised up on a platform for greater prominence.

Above: *A collection of terracotta pots planted with spring flowers has brought this dull brick wall to life early in the season. Replace the bulbs with bright annuals for the summer.*

Right: *A quiet corner of the border can become a place for relaxation and contemplation if you add a simple seat, such as this stone bench, among the lupins, choisya, spiraea and violas.*

Left: This tiny backyard is packed with interest thanks to a clever combination of plants and features with a green-blue theme. Amassing plants and accessories like this creates a sense of escape to a secret place.

Clipped hedges on this scale can take years to accomplish, but quicker-growing hedges or climbers trained up supports can achieve a similar effect.

Below: A classical statue on an imposing pedestal not only adds height to this traditional setting, but also looks great against the dark green background. The statue is essential to the whole impact of the formal vista edged with clipped box and yew.

Left: Use plenty of small pots planted with bright, summer-flowering plants, such as these geraniums and pelargoniums. Push the pots close together to make a brave display around the garden or on the patio.

Coping with a narrow garden

Below: *Clever use of curves and strategically placed focal points distract attention from the length and narrowness of this typical problem site.*

It is a typical town or terrace garden: the long narrow strip, bordered on either side by walls or fences, often with no access other than through the house or across a neighbor's garden, which can make bringing in bulky materials and machinery difficult. The first thing to do is to break up the length of the plot in some way and get rid of that tunnel effect. You can do this by dividing the garden into new areas or outdoor 'rooms', using screens or trellis covered in climbing plants, so that part of the garden is hidden from view. This garden shows a more traditional layout, and the problem is tackled slightly differently, by providing something of special interest at the far end of the plot, which not only shortens the focal length of the overall view, but also helps to give an impression of width. The design avoids any straight lines, especially down the length of the site, which would only serve to emphasize the limited boundaries. Traditional flower borders follow a curvaceous profile and are broken on the one side by an informal pool that makes an important focal point and adds a sense of breadth in the center of the plot. Rather than a path to link the patio area, which would only introduce longitudinal straight lines, stepping stones follow a more random course. Trees are always useful for making a tall, natural screen to disguise the true length of a garden. Here, a specimen tree screens part of the end patio. The generous, gently curved patio near the house provides a convenient and stylish seating and eating area.

Terraced houses can cause garden problems. Plots tend to be narrow and access to the garden is often limited.

With neighbors on either side, boundary fences must provide privacy and security, yet make an attractive background to a long garden plot.

A major feature at the end of the garden helps to square up a narrow shape and provides a diversionary focal point.

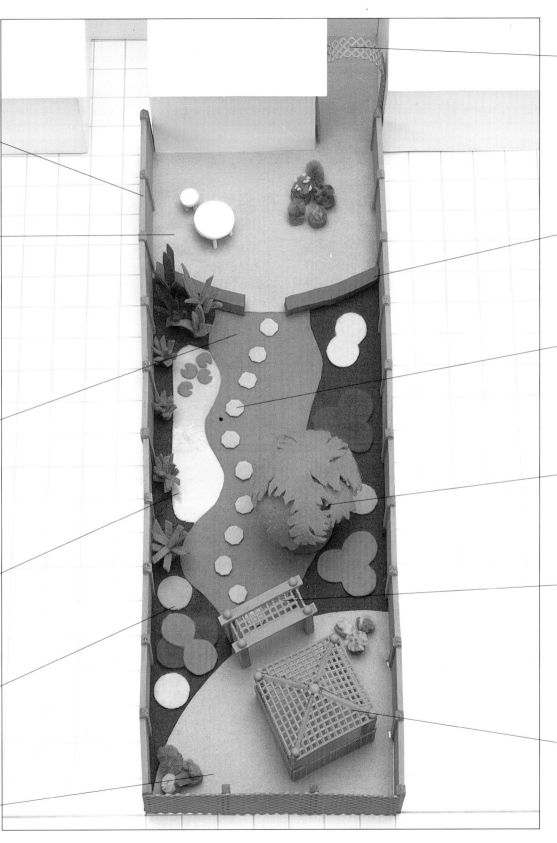

Decorative close-boarded fence panels provide shelter and privacy around the patio. A good alternative would be stout trellis covered in evergreen creepers.

A paved area provides a clean, dry approach to the house and somewhere to sit in all seasons. Colored paving slabs, a pattern of bricks or random stone would all be appropriate here, depending on how formal you want it to look.

A pleasant grassy area winds its way down the garden following the course of informal flower borders, yet still maintains an easy-to-mow lawn with no awkward corners.

An informal kidney-shaped pond is a good opportunity to introduce an area of lush planting and exciting moisture-loving species with their dramatic variety of foliage shapes.

Informal beds planted with colorful perennials create a seasonal display to view from various angles of the garden.

Curves and undulations soften and disguise the hard lines of the plot.

A decorative arch makes a feature out of an awkward side passage and helps to conceal the utility area.

A low wall makes a natural boundary between patio and garden without obscuring the view and adds a slightly formal touch. You could use bricks or blocks to match the paving surface.

Stepping stones have a far less formal appearance than a path. Use up any paving units left over from building the patio.

A small specimen tree creates a useful focal point as well as height and seasonal interest. A Japanese maple, a crab apple or a dogwood would all be suitable.

This pergola makes a leafy entrance to the lower patio and also links the planting areas.

An ornamental gazebo on the second patio adds height and interest in a position where most gardens have run out of inspiration. It makes an excellent focal point and a shady place to sit and view the garden from a new angle in hot weather.

Garden design on a grand scale

In many ways, a large garden is more difficult to design than a small one. There is all that space to fill without the limitations imposed by a restrictive shape and size. The way to tackle it is not to be overwhelmed by the scale of the task, but to divide the plot into new, more manageable areas and then to deal with each one in turn. If planned carefully, these areas should interconnect to form a logical whole, making an attractive and interesting environment to explore and enjoy. Here, a large water feature provides spectacular views and reflections from the house, and an extensive decked leisure area overlooks the water and includes a hot tub and comfortable seating. Hidden from the rest of the garden is a well-organized herb and vegetable plot to supply a keen cook with home-grown ingredients. A second patio beneath a large pergola offers shady seating and a separate barbecue and eating facility.

Below: This extensive site includes many exciting and practical ideas, yet it is not difficult to maintain. Distinct areas are cleverly interlocked to give the site a strong identity as a whole.

Thinking big

If you plan a pool, make it a large one, maybe on several levels and incorporating, say, a fountain, falls or water sculpture. Include islands or a boggy marsh area in a large informal pond. On an extensive patio area try changes of level, plus a range of seating and storage. A change of materials over large areas adds variety and interest.

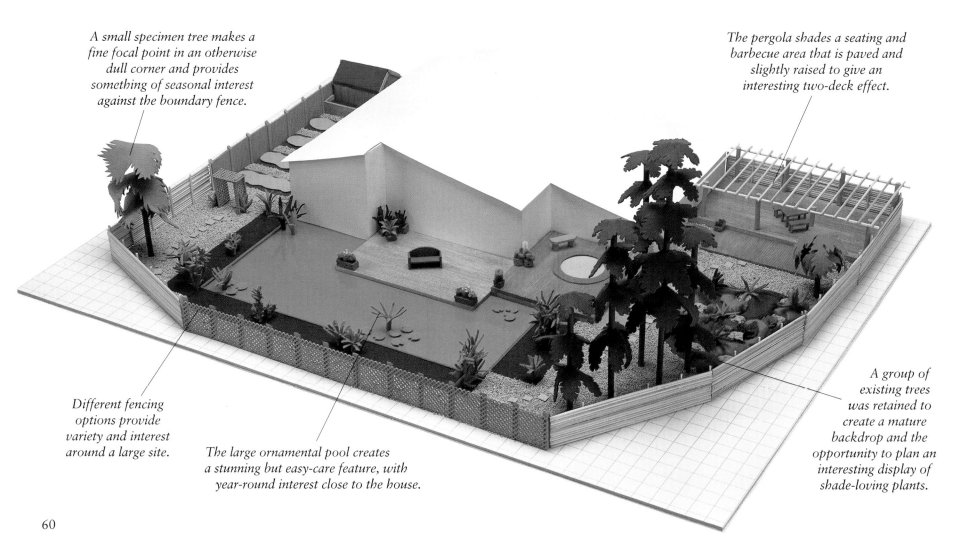

A small specimen tree makes a fine focal point in an otherwise dull corner and provides something of seasonal interest against the boundary fence.

The pergola shades a seating and barbecue area that is paved and slightly raised to give an interesting two-deck effect.

Different fencing options provide variety and interest around a large site.

The large ornamental pool creates a stunning but easy-care feature, with year-round interest close to the house.

A group of existing trees was retained to create a mature backdrop and the opportunity to plan an interesting display of shade-loving plants.

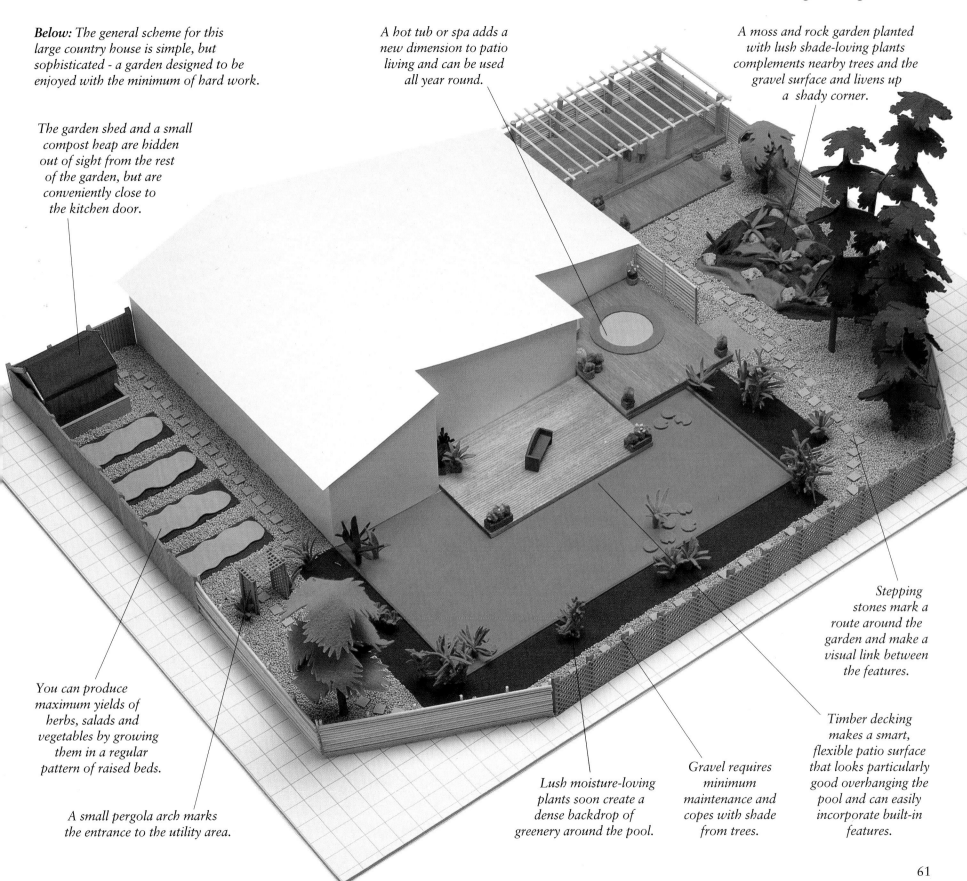

Below: *The general scheme for this large country house is simple, but sophisticated - a garden designed to be enjoyed with the minimum of hard work.*

The garden shed and a small compost heap are hidden out of sight from the rest of the garden, but are conveniently close to the kitchen door.

A hot tub or spa adds a new dimension to patio living and can be used all year round.

A moss and rock garden planted with lush shade-loving plants complements nearby trees and the gravel surface and livens up a shady corner.

You can produce maximum yields of herbs, salads and vegetables by growing them in a regular pattern of raised beds.

A small pergola arch marks the entrance to the utility area.

Lush moisture-loving plants soon create a dense backdrop of greenery around the pool.

Gravel requires minimum maintenance and copes with shade from trees.

Stepping stones mark a route around the garden and make a visual link between the features.

Timber decking makes a smart, flexible patio surface that looks particularly good overhanging the pool and can easily incorporate built-in features.

Part Two

CHOOSING AND USING PLANTS

The hard landscaping, the skeleton of a garden design that was laid out in part one, is essential to success and creates the basic look. But it is the plants that breathe life and ever-changing interest into your scheme. To ensure that plants grow well and with the minimum amount of care, choose varieties to suit the site; assess each one according to its soil, shade or sun requirements and then consider its height, spread and habit. For that lush, professional look, also aim for a good variety of colors, shapes and textures within your planting scheme. Remember that foliage is as important as flowers and can offer just as many variations. Consider seasonal interest - the best gardens have something on display right through the year. Finally, bear in mind that plants have a practical purpose, as well as a decorative one, be they climbers to clothe the pergola or trellis, ground cover plants for covering bare patches of soil and binding slopes, or shrubs and trees to add height and body to the general plan. Trailing varieties of plants will soften the edges of containers and hanging baskets and there are dramatic architectural plants for bold displays, rampant growers for informal schemes and delicate scents and color for special intimate areas - in fact, a plant for every purpose.

Left: Color and shape in complete harmony.   **Right:** *The vivid blooms of* Meconopsis grandis.

A palette of annual flowers

Choosing and growing annuals is creative, it's fun and the plants are relatively short-lived and inexpensive, so you need not worry about making mistakes. You have a fabulous palette of flower types and colors at your fingertips, to be coordinated and contrasted in beds and borders, pots, tubs, baskets and troughs, and because they only last a single, if glorious, season, you can try out new combinations and effects every year. If you grow plants from seed, the choice of colors and types is even wider. You can choose exactly the shades you want and try out the latest introductions, whether that be a range of subtle pastels, double forms or interesting petal markings. Many annuals, such as petunias, antirrhinums, geraniums and impatiens, are available in a mixture of carefully selected shades, but you can also buy many single colors to mix and match your own, more subtle effects. Often a two- or three-color combination is the most effective in containers, remembering to maintain a good contrast of heights and shapes. You might go for a hot Mediterranean mix of bold primaries, a more sophisticated blend of golds and blues, oranges and creams, or simply all-white for a really special effect. Painting with plants really comes into its own if you are planning a traditional bedding scheme where the plants are arranged in geometric patterns, even letters and words, picked out in the different colors. It is vital to prepare the bed thoroughly, making sure it is free from weeds, and sketch out the design in advance, using string or a sprinkling of sand.

Carpet-forming alyssum adds lighter tones

Tiny white violas for hanging baskets and pots

Some of the larger pansies have attractive 'faces'

French marigolds - a wide range of single colors

Begonias appear in many forms and colors

Marigolds offer a range of strong colors

French marigolds - in many patterns

Brilliant orange gazanias for beds and tubs

Marigold flowers - small but plentiful

French marigolds, Tagetes, have bright green foliage and eye-catching flowers

Yellow daisylike flowers brighten up beds and borders

Impatiens - a mass of single or double blooms in many colors and patterns

The color range of pansies extends into these lovely purple shades

Densely-headed verbena adds strong color

Petunias are available in plain and striped colors

A yellow eye gives hot pink begonias striking appeal

Alyssum is also available in pink and mauve color combinations

Pansies with strong color contrasts add extra impact

Dahlias offer fine petal configurations and splendid colors

Pansies also offer velvet textures combined with deep colors

Above: Unexpected contrasts of color can be used to create a flowery focal point, such as this splash of gold among a sea of pinks and mauves.

Below: Here, the brighter colors of mixed annuals are reserved for the patio, while the rest of the garden is low key with a mostly green scheme.

Annuals - a foliage palette

When choosing annuals, it is sometimes easy to focus on the lovely flowers and forget that many varieties have interesting and colorful foliage, too. You should deliberately add a few exciting leaf shapes and colors to your arrangements in order to introduce some variety and texture. This is particularly important with hanging baskets, windowboxes and other containers positioned at eye level. Some plants can offer both striking flowers and foliage; there are zonal geraniums, for example; the stripes, spots and borders of begonias; the feathery, if rather pungent, leaves of the *Tagetes* family, or the large lily-pad-like leaves of the nasturtium. Other annuals are worth growing for their striking foliage alone, because their shape and/or color can make a significant contribution to a planting scheme. The lacy, silver leaves of *Senecio maritima,* for example, are a long-standing favorite for adding highlights to tub and bedding schemes; also popular is the more dramatic *Coleus blumei,* with its strongly patterned leaves in deep reds and greens. The castor-oil plant, *Ricinus communis,* is often grown as an annual, its large, hand-shaped leaves adding an exotic touch. The variety 'Impala' is particularly impressive, providing a dramatic display of deeply cut bronze leaves. For a softer look, the light green feathery effect of the summer cypress, *Kochia scoparia,* has the advantage of turning red at the end of the summer. Another useful foliage annual with a lightening effect that looks superb among your container and bedding plants, is snow-in-summer, *Euphorbia marginata,* which grows fast to make an attractive small bush of bright green and white variegated leaves. And why not try the spiky, striped foliage of ornamental sweetcorn *(Zea mays),* which is available in various forms.

Useful feathery foliage of Argyranthemum frutescens *'Jamaica Primrose'*

Delicately variegated Lamium maculatum *'Pink Pearl'*

Cineraria maritima *adds a light touch in beds and borders*

Verbena leaves - a good foil for bright blooms

Bedding begonias

Euonymus fortunei *'Emerald Gaiety'*

Sempervivum *'Brownii'*

Feathery bronze fennel adds interest

Golden foliage adds a splash of sunshine to your color scheme. This is golden marjoram.

Lamium maculatum 'Gold Nuggets' has a light freshness useful for lifting darker plants

Pelargonium 'Mrs. Quilter'

The golden variegation of Euonymus fortunei 'Emerald 'n' Gold'

Pelargonium 'Happy Thoughts' has attractive creamy yellow centers

Feathery feverfew (Tanacetum parthenium) is always useful among annual arrangements

Above: Euphorbia marginata, or snow-in-summer, is popular for its bushy mass of bright green-and-white marked leaves. They have a refreshing effect among other annual plants.

Above: The fast-growing burning bush, Kochia scoparia *f.* trichophylla, has light green, feathery leaves and grows no more than 24in(60cm) tall. It also has bright red fall color.

Above: Coleus are specially grown for their colorful foliage, available in a wide range of unusual shapes and patterns. Remove the tiny flowers.

A border in white, silver and blue

The discipline of using a controlled color scheme can really pay off in the smaller garden or backyard, or even among your pots on the patio, where a riot of too many summer colors can sometimes appear crowded and somewhat claustrophobic. If you restrict your choice to a subtle blend of shades, such as the new pastels or, as here, a cool combination of whites, silvers and blues, the effect is automatically one of sophistication and restfulness, the ideal antidote to stress for those with busy lifestyles. With a limited scheme such as this, a good variety of different foliage shapes and textures is just as important as color, and once you start making your selection you will be surprised at the choice available for creating interesting contrasts within your color band. Remember, too, that plant foliage can provide fine colors that are just as effective as flower colors and they will last longer as well. Also useful are variegated foliage forms, whose stripes, borders and splashes achieve the desired effect without presenting a block of solid color.

A scheme like this also needs careful planning with respect to any surrounding ornamental features, boundaries and backdrops. A red brick wall or dark-stained fence would be inappropriate and spoil the general effect of sophisticated coolness. Equally, such a light-colored theme would be lost against a white background. Keep the surrounds and nearby structural features in coordinating shades - even if you have to paint or stain them using special stone or timber paint - and you will achieve a very professional and pleasing result.

Geranium sylvaticum
‘Amy Doncaster’

Veronica
gentianoides

Dactylis glomerata
‘Variegata’

Saxifraga densa
(Mossy saxifrage)

Stachys byzantina
'Lamb's Ear'

Disporum sessile
'Variegatum'

Iris (dwarf) 'Tinkerbell'

Iris (dwarf bearded)
'Lilli-White'

Hieracium lanatum

Phlox subulata
'G.F. Wilson'

Salvia argentea

Above: A wonderful all-white scheme shows just what can be done with a single shade of color. Hosta crispula, *with its white variegated leaves, adds texture and interest among the white clustered flowers of a viburnum, with tulips 'White Parrot' and 'Blizzard' for some extra seasonal display.*

Veronica peduncularis
'Georgia Blue'

Experimenting with themed borders

Choosing a deliberate scheme of only one or two colors in your beds and borders can be an enjoyable and rewarding exercise. Collecting species and varieties with leaves, stems or flowers in your chosen shade, and the excitement of discovering an unusual plant in the right colors adds a new dimension to gardening and puts it on a par with interior design. Whatever color or colors you choose, they are usually offset by the natural background of green leaves, although of course, a selection of plants with foliage or variegation in your chosen color adds new shades and textures. If you restrict the color of foliage, say to silver or yellow/gold, be prepared for a rather two-dimensional effect. Even if you do not relish the idea of limiting yourself to a narrow color band, it pays to plan your borders carefully with respect to color, as well as height and shape. Take the advice of the renowned garden designer Gertrude Jekyll and use blocks or bands of different shades along the length of the border; she liked to start with cool colors such as blues and silvers and ran through mauves and purple to the hotter reds and oranges. The effect is both subtle and stunning.

Below left: *A herbaceous border with a purple theme uses both flowers and foliage.* Geranium sanguineum, Knautia macedonia, Salvia superba *and* Lathyrus latifolius *all feature here.*

Below right: *A bright red border is unusual but dramatic, and creates an instant and unavoidable focal point. Plenty of dark green is required to offset the brightness of the color.*

The border includes 'Bishop of Llandaff' dahlias and nicotianas.

Planting for effect

Restricting the color scheme is useful for creating certain effects with a practical purpose. Brighten up an otherwise dark corner with a combination of sunny yellow and orange, add excitement to a dull garden with splashes of red. Or make yours a place to relax with a mixture of soft pinks and mauves.

Right: *In this pretty pink scheme, roses, Achillea and Lavatera are planted in a profusion of color and shape, rather than being arranged in individual clumps. It is easy on the eye and simple to copy.*

Below left: *A planting combination of yellow and orange brightens the flower border without looking too garish. There are plenty of plants with golden flowers or foliage to choose from.*

Below right: *Yellow adds a splash of sunlight to a shady corner. This display of tulips, cowslips and hellebores is full of the early promise of spring.*

Heathers for all-year-round beds

Heathers can be useful for providing color and interest in selected parts of the garden all year round. They are evergreen and usually make dense clumps or cushions of good ground-covering foliage, although there are a few types that can grow as high as 20ft(6m). Both flowers and foliage are highly colored and different types can be spring, summer, fall or winter-flowering, so it is possible to plan a continuous display using different genera and varieties. Foliage colors vary from every shade of green to gold and yellow. Flowers might be white, pink, purple or mauve, and come in bicolored as well as double forms. Many heathers are fully hardy. A few species are lime-tolerant, but as a rule, most heathers prefer an acid soil, a rich, well-drained position and plenty of sunshine. They are ideal for providing interest on slopes and within alpine gardens, or in suitable beds and borders, either mixed with other plants or en masse to create a special colorful display of their own. To prevent the plants becoming leggy, prune them lightly after flowering. There are three main groups of heathers. The largest is *Erica*, which includes summer and winter-flowering varieties. *Daboecia* has two species, both of which are summer flowering. The third group, *Calluna*, has only one species, *Calluna vulgaris*, but it does include a great many cultivars that flower from midsummer through to late fall.

Erica *x* darleyensis *'Arthur Johnson' has lilac-pink flowers in winter.*

Calluna vulgaris *'Silver Queen' has dark lilac-pink flowers.*

Daboecia cantabrica *'Atropurpurea' has single or double mauve flowers.*

Calluna vulgaris *'Beoley Silver' has silver and white flowers.*

Calluna vulgaris *'Gold Haze' has gold foliage and white flowers.*

The green leaves of Calluna vulgaris *'Spring Cream' have cream tips in spring.*

Daboecia *x* scotica *'Silverwells' is an evergreen that flowers from late spring until mid fall.*

Erica cinerea *'Domino' has a long flowering period from spring to fall.*

Calluna vulgaris *'Silver Knight' has gray leaves and pink flowers.*

Erica *x* darleyensis *'Jenny Porter' makes reddish shoots in spring and has winter flowers.*

Above: *This colorful, all-seasons planting bed consists only of heathers and conifers yet produces a densely covered landscape of shape and color.*

Below: *The dense mass of evergreen foliage and purple coloring of Daboecia cantabrica* '*Atropurpurea*' *makes useful permanent ground cover in beds and borders. A single green dwarf conifer adds a contrasting note.*

Calluna vulgaris *'Kirby White' has white flowers in late summer.*

Calluna vulgaris *'Golden Carpet' has golden foliage that turns red-orange in winter.*

Using variegated plants

Variegated plants provide the patterns in our gardens; the spots and stripes, the splashes, splotches and borders. Similar markings in flower blooms give them a rather exotic appearance, but the massed effect of variegated foliage is more like a richly patterned piece of cloth. It contributes an area of special interest and, where the markings are white, cream, yellow or gold, it creates light and the effect of dappled sunlight, which can be a useful design device in dull or dark corners. There is an infinite variety of variegations to choose from; stripes both wide and narrow, horizontal and vertical; tiny polkadots and random splashes, rims and borders. Where each leaf may have every vein picked out in a contrasting color, such as the silver net-leaf, *Fittonia argyroneura*, the effect can be strikingly intricate. Others, like the stiff green spears of *Sansevieria trifasciata* 'Laurentii', might feature several effects; its leaves are edged in gold with dark zigzagged horizontal stripes.

Range of colors

You will find variegated plants amongst annuals and perennials, shrubs, trees, reeds, rushes and grasses, in every shade of green from the palest lime to dark velvet green. There are browns and bronzes, creams and whites, yellows and golds, reds, russets and even pinks and purples.

Phalaris arundinacea *'Feesey'*

Pieris *'Flaming Silver'*

Heuchera *'Pewter Moon'*

Heuchera sanguinea *'Snow Storm'*

Azalea *'Salmon's Leap'*

Right: *This garden makes excellent use of variegated plants where golds and silvers have been used to lighten the stronger colors and shapes of a dense arrangement of shrubs.*

Keeping variegation

Remember that in order to maintain the variegated effect of foliage, it is important to cut out any rogue stems or leaves that revert to green in summer.

Ilex aquifolium
'Argentea Marginata'
(female)

Iris pseudacorus
'Variegata'

Aegopodium podagraria
'Variegatum'

Hosta fortunei
'Francee'

Houttuynia cordata
'Chameleon'

Aromatic-leaved shrubs

Scent is a wonderful asset in the garden and you should give it as much consideration as shape and color when drawing up your final plant list. Many summer flowers contribute to an overall potpourri of scent, and there is a wide choice of climbers with blooms that provide sweet smells in winter, as well as during the summer. Many shrubs also have scented foliage, which can add another dimension to the heady fragrance of a well-planned garden. Whereas the scent of flowers is sweet and sometimes even sickly, aromatic foliage tends to be pungent and spicy. These are the plants that you should position near paths and walkways, where you are likely to brush against them and release that rich aroma. Some of the prostrate forms of herbs, such as thyme and chamomile, can even be planted in the cracks between paving stones or in seats, where treading or sitting on the plants does them no harm and only intensifies their effect. Alternatively, you might reserve your aromatic shrubs for strategic positions close to the patio, or even put them in raised beds, where they can be appreciated and handled at closer quarters. Many are evergreen so you can enjoy them right through the year, while others offer scented flowers as well as foliage, thus providing excellent 'garden value'. Others have leaves or stems that might be collected and dried for potpourris or sweet bags to give pleasure around the house as well as in the garden.

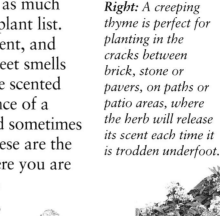

Right: A creeping thyme is perfect for planting in the cracks between brick, stone or pavers, on paths or patio areas, where the herb will release its scent each time it is trodden underfoot.

Left: This garden has been designed for the visually impaired, and features raised beds of santolina, sage and lilac to touch and smell. Wooden edging makes a guide rail around the garden.

Above: The evergreen Mexican orange blossom, Choisya ternata, *has aromatic glossy leaves, as well as pretty scented flowers. It needs plenty of sun and a sheltered site to flourish.*

Choisya ternata

Lavandula stoechas
pendunculata
(French lavender)

Santolina chamaecyparissus
'Pretty Carol'

Laurus nobilis
(sweet bay)

More scents to savor

Aloysia triphylla/Lippia citriodora
(Lemon verbena)
Artemisia abrotanum
(Southernwood)
Hyssopus officinalis *(Hyssop)*
Lindera benzoin *(Spicebush)*
Myrtus communis
(Common myrtle)
Salvia officinalis
(Garden sage)

Rosmarinus officinalis
'Primley Blue' (rosemary)

Helichrysum serotinum
(curry plant)

The alpine garden

Alpine plants are naturally adapted to harsh conditions and extremely poor, free-draining soil, which makes them useful for certain difficult sites around the garden where other plants would find it hard to flourish. Most alpines prefer plenty of sunshine, although there are a very few that will tolerate shade or partial shade. Alpines are a perfect choice for areas of poor or stony soil, for slopes or for natural stone walls, where the plants can be grown along the top or in pockets of soil between the stones. While the plants themselves are often stunted or dwarfed by the stringent conditions of their natural habitat, alpine flowers are among the most beautiful and can be exquisitely delicate. To grow a larger selection, you will have to create a rock or alpine garden; carefully constructed and patiently maintained until established, this is a feature that will reward you with a spectacular collection of plants.

The tricky part is making a suitable arrangement of rocks and boulders to resemble as closely as possible a natural rocky outcrop. The site should ideally be open and sunny, with plenty of stones and rubble worked into the soil to improve drainage. A grassy slope or a built-up area behind a pool is often perfect. The stones should be positioned according to their natural strata, embedded in the soil and tilted slightly backwards to allow any moisture to drain off their surface towards the roots of the plants. It helps to position the larger rocks or boulders first, but be prepared for some strenuous trial and error until you are totally happy with the result. Do not cover the whole area with rocks - leave some parts bare for plants.

Aquilegia akitensis

Ranunculus gramineus

Phlox 'Daniel's Cushion'

Dianthus myrtinervius

Erigeron pyrenaicus

Anthyllis vulneraria

Helianthemum
'Georgeham'

Right: *The perennial* Lewisia
cotyledon *hybrids are an attractive
group of evergreen alpines that create
a large clump of fleshy leaves arranged
in rosettes. Clusters of pink or purple
flowers on long stems rise up from the
rosettes in early summer.*

Thymus
'Anderson's Gold'

Saxifraga
'Triumph'

Sedum
'Cape Blanco'

Sempervivum x
calcaratum

Sempervivum
'Red'

Hypericum
polyphyllum

Arenaria caespitosa
'Aurea'

Iberis sempervirens
'Little Gem'

Phlox douglasii
'Rosea'

Oxalis
adenophylla

79

Planting alpines

You can plant pot-grown alpine or rock plants at any time between early spring and fall, although the earlier you plant them, the longer they will have to become established over the summer. Weeds are the scourge of rock gardens, so ensure that the soil is as weed-free as possible before you plant and continue to weed the area conscientiously until the plants are established. Aim for a good variety of different alpine plant types to soften the edges of rocks and boulders and make the feature look as natural as possible. It is possible to have something of interest right through the year, with spring, summer or late-season flowering varieties and plants with interesting evergreen foliage. Dwarf conifers are useful for adding height and winter interest. Many alpines have a creeping or trailing habit and can be trained between the stones; try alyssum or the pretty spreading *Geranium orientalitibeticum*, the brilliant mass of blue flowers produced by *Lithodora diffusa* 'Heavenly Blue' or snow-in-summer, *Cerastium tomentosum*, which makes a carpet of silver-gray leaves and tiny white flowers. Other alpines make a compact dome or cushion, such as the miniature moss campion, *Silene acaulis,* with its tiny pink spring flowers, bright yellow *Draba rigida* and the wonderful tight, dark-green rosettes of *Sagina boydii*. Then there are fleshy-leaved rock plants - sedums sempervivums and raoulias - whose whorls and rosettes cling to rock or scree. Do not allow plants to become waterlogged in winter.

Below: A mulch of gravel or stone chippings between alpine plants helps to conserve moisture and suppress weeds. It also prevents the surface of the soil becoming so hard that it is difficult to break up.

Saxifraga 'Stansfieldii'

Phlox subulata 'Amazing Grace'

Cotyledon simplicifolia

Saxifraga x primulaize

Sedum spurium 'Dragon's Blood'

Minuartia circassica

Polemonium
caeruleum album

Lychnis alpina rosea

Primula sieboldii

Phlox subulata
'G F Wilson'

Dianthus
'Betty Norton'

Primula *sp.*

Ajuga reptans
'Variegata'

Viola
'Molly Sanderson'

Sedum purpureum

Sempervivum
'Morning Glory'

Thymus serpyllum
'Goldstream'

Gentiana verna

Ranunculus montanus
'Molten Gold'

Ground cover for shady areas

Shady areas in the garden and city backyard are traditionally the most difficult to plant up successfully. Too often, that dry desert beneath the trees or dank stretch along the wall is given last-resort treatment with a touch of hard landscaping. This is not only unimaginative, but wastes an area that could otherwise put on a good display. Choose the right kind of plants, those that originate from woodland and other naturally shady areas, and they will flourish where other specimens turn sickly and die. Seek out good ground-covering plants that will eventually knit together to create a patchwork of shapes and colors. Many such plants have interesting or dramatic foliage and delicate or exotic-looking flowers that make them well worth including in your scheme. Feathery ferns and plants that grow from bulbs or corms are often first choice for a shady site. While ferns are more usually associated with damp areas, there are several species that will tolerate drier conditions too; *Nephrolepis exaltata* or *Polypodium vulgare*, for example. Dry shade can be the most difficult to tackle, yet there are spreading shrubs and perennial plants that will tolerate such conditions; *Daphne laureola, Ilex aquifolium* and *Alchemilla mollis* are just a few. For damp sites choose rhododendrons, hostas and primulas, as well as many other lovely woodland shrubs, climbers and perennials that need little care.

Bergenia cordifolia *'Purpurea' makes a clump of large round leaves with clusters of pink flowers in winter.*

Hosta *x* tardiana *'Halcyon' has narrow dark green leaves and clusters of lilac trumpet flowers in late summer.*

Dryopteris filix-mas *(male fern) produces attractive arching green fronds*

Ajuga reptans *'Atropurpurea' (purple bugle) is a spreading evergreen with bronze-purple leaves.*

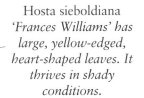

Hosta sieboldiana 'Frances Williams' has large, yellow-edged, heart-shaped leaves. It thrives in shady conditions.

Right: *The carefully chosen plants in this raised peat bed have produced dense ground cover that reduces moisture loss and the need to weed. Bark chips make a suitable mulch.*

Below: *Here, shade-loving species, such as ferns, mosses and hostas, have been allowed to create a lush display of foliage around a small but highly decorative waterspout.*

Alchemilla erythropoda *makes a good perennial ground cover that tolerates most soil types.*

Ground cover for sunny areas

Below: The later-flowering clematis hybrids guarantee a carpet of delightful color from midsummer until the first frost.

Good ground cover can be important in sunny areas, providing interest beneath and in front of taller plants, and reducing moisture loss from the soil. Most ground cover plants are mound- or carpet-forming and spread quickly, but until they have matured, mulch bare areas of soil with bark chips or a similar organic material. Select plants according to the particular situation: *Aubretia, Alyssum montanum*, sedums and saxifrages suit stony slopes and alpine areas, for example. Within beds and borders you might prefer perennials and shrubs, such as *Cotoneaster*, heathers, spreading *Centaurea montana* or spring-flowering *Lamium maculatum*, with its mat-forming, softly striped leaves. For strong evergreen cover, many junipers provide a year-round colorful display in a sunny position with dry, well-drained soil. The more prostrate forms are best and are available in grays and greens. Do not forget the value of climbers as ground covering plants; various clematis will do well in this situation, or allow *Lathyrus latifolius*, the everlasting pea, to make a tangle of narrow green foliage and purple flower spikes.

Hebe topiana is an evergreen shrub that prefers well-drained soil in full sun.

Cotoneaster congestus *makes a dense mound of evergreen foliage, small pink flowers and red fruits.*

Geum x borisii 'Werner Arends' *produces a mass of orange flowers in summer.*

Geranium sanguineum *combines attractive, deeply cut green foliage with a mass of pink summer flowers.*

Left: Centaurea montana *is a spreading perennial that produces a carpet of light green, pointed leaves, studded with large, purple, thistlelike flowerheads in early summer.*

Right: Cushion-forming ground cover plants for sunny sites are often a mass of tiny flowers all summer. Here, alyssum and saxifrage mingle together to create a patchwork effect.

Sasaella masamuneana 'Albostriata' (bamboo)

Juniperus horizontalis 'Blue Chip' is a creeping juniper that makes a thick mat of blue-green foliage.

Potentilla crantzii 'Goldrausch' is an alpine with golden spring flowers.

Nepeta nervosa (catmint) makes a clump of pointed aromatic leaves and a mass of small blue flowers.

Plants for boggy soils

If constructing a pond or pool is not practical in your garden, but you would still like to grow a selection of dramatic moisture-loving plants, you could always include a bog or marsh area in your design plans. The ideal site would be a badly drained hollow on a clay-based soil or where the water table is close to the surface. However, if this is not available, you can always recreate the effect by excavating to about 14in(35cm), lining the area with punctured butyl pond liner and filling it with moist, humus-rich soil. If space is really limited, you can create a successful miniature bog garden in an old sink or cut down barrel with drainage holes drilled in the bottom. This could be free-standing or partially sunk into the ground and surrounded by pebbles or boulders. Lush, moisture-loving plants are among the most exciting species you can exhibit in the garden, and providing you can keep the soil damp at all times, they will flourish with very little maintenance. Aim for a good variety of shapes and sizes.

Iris sibirica
'Sparkling Rose'

Peltiphyllum
peltatum

Aquilegia
alpina

Geranium sanguineum *'Glenluce'*

Left: *Clump-forming* Hosta *'Halcyon' is a typical bold and colorful moisture-loving plant. It has attractive heart-shaped, gray-blue leaves and clusters of mauve flowers on long stems in midsummer.*

These magnificent leaves can grow up to 5ft(1.5m) across.

Below: *Few garden plants are as dramatic and architectural as* Gunnera manicata. *It will thrive in sun or shade in damp soil at the edge of the pool.*

The conical structure at the center of the plant is the flower spike.

Above: *Even a small pond or bog garden can play host to a wonderful variety of dramatic marginal and bog species since these are plants that thrive when planted close together.*

Conifers for every situation

Conifers have acquired rather a poor reputation in gardens, where all too often the wrong size or color species has been chosen or too many trees have been planted in an inappropriate position, with gloomy and frequently overpowering results. In fact, conifers include a wonderful range of sculptural shapes and astonishing colors which, if planned carefully, can be valuable additions to your garden plan. Most are evergreen, which means all-year interest and something to brighten up the garden in winter. Colors include blues, grays and silvers, greens, purples, bronze and gold. There is also a wide selection of dwarf or slow-growing varieties which are very useful for adding a sense of permanence and maturity to tubs and containers or to alpine gardens. Conifers also make a quick and excellent screen if you are considering a hedge. The secret is to make those shapes and colors work for you.

Conifer shapes

Upright and tall, narrow, conical species are useful for adding height. Other types might create a natural pyramid, ball or dome for formal effects without the need for regular clipping. Yet others have a spreading habit that makes useful evergreen ground cover. Keep groups varied in size and shape. Prune evergreen hedges so that they do not become too dominant.

Juniperus squamata 'Holger'

Thuja orientalis 'Elegantissima'

Chamaecyparis lawsoniana 'Emerald'

Chamaecyparis lawsoniana 'Snow White'

Pinus mugo 'Humpy'

Picea abies 'Wills Zwerg'

Chamaecyparis lawsoniana 'Green Globe'

Chamaecyparis lawsoniana
'Ellwood's Pillar'

This standard form of Chamaecyparis lawsoniana 'Nymph' is produced by painstakingly removing all the side growth.

Pinus leucodermis
'Compact Gem'

Chamaecyparis lawsoniana
'Ellwood's Gold'

Above: *A stylish arrangement of conifers suits a large island bed, where you can blend greens and golds in varying heights and shapes to provide a virtually maintenance-free, year-round display of color and interest.*

Juniperus squamata
'Holger'

Picea glauca
'Alberta Globe'

Picea mariana
'Nana'

Picea pungens
'Glauca Globosa'

Climbers - the perfect cover-up

Climbing plants are wonderfully versatile; they are a gardener's equivalent of paint, paper and fabric when it comes to design. Not only do they offer interesting, often stunning, foliage, flowers and fragrance, but they can also be trained or entwined over virtually any surface to provide a carpet of ground cover, a hanging curtain or an overhead canopy wherever you choose. There are sun-loving and shade-tolerant varieties, evergreens and berried varieties for winter interest, and flowers for every season. Most climbing plants grow quickly - some remarkably quickly - so you can achieve some kind of effect within a single season. Use them to add height to your scheme and to soften arches, walkways and pergolas. Climbers are masters of disguise, too. With a firmly fixed trellis or training wires you can easily liven up a wall or fence, while stronger, free-standing supports act as screens or dividers within the garden to hide the shed or utility area, or simply to create more intimate spaces. Climbing plants are perfect for quick decorative effects; you can train them up ornamental supports such as pyramids, domes or spirals, which look perfect in tubs and containers. Alternatively, use wire hoops and arches to create imaginative flowering bowers, enclosures and covered walks.

Lonicera brownii *'Dropmore Scarlet' produces small but stunning scented red flowers in summer. The oval leaves are blue-green in color.*

Lonicera periclymenum, *the common honeysuckle, or woodbine, is perfect for rustic arches and other country-style features where you need a vigorous climber with heavily scented flowers.*

Clematis montana *'Mayleen' is one of a vigorous group of climbers perfect for smothering large buildings or among the branches of a tree, where it produces a mass of flowers in late spring.*

The Russian vine produces racemes of fluffy white flowers.

Tropaeolum tuberosum *'Ken Aslet'* has blue-green leaves and tiny, trumpetlike red and orange flowers from midsummer until fall.

Polygonum baldschuanicum, *the Russian vine, grows so quickly that it will screen a pergola or building within a single season.*

Solanum crispum *'Glasnevin', a scrambling, semi-evergreen climber, grows quickly to make a good screen of oval leaves. Clusters of purple flowers appear in summer.*

Above: *Vigorous scrambling climbers, such as Solanum crispum 'Glasnevin', soon cover a structure in a mass of foliage and flowers.*

Below: *Few climbers do such an efficient cover-up as Polygonum baldschuanicum. It is ideal for hiding eyesores, such as sheds and garages.*

Choosing climbing plants

The choice of climbing plants is vast and each one has its merits, be it flowers, foliage, fruits, or a combination of assets that make it worth considering. Luckily, even the smallest garden or backyard has room for several species - this is vertical gardening at its best. Evergreen climbers are perfect where you want all-year-round cover and interest, but only a few, including *Jasminum polyanthum* and the unusual *Hoya australis*, with its glossy foliage and starlike flowers, produce the spectacular flowers and scent we expect in the perfect garden. A deciduous variety can be useful where a little extra light and space are welcome during the darker months, say under a pergola or arch. Ivies are an obvious evergreen favorite, with many foliage shapes and colors to choose from, including golds and purples as well as variegated forms. Other interesting evergreen climbers include the pretty kangaroo vine, *Cissus antarctica,* and the fast-growing, glossy, heart leaf, *Philodendron scandens.* As well as the classic climbers without which no garden seems complete - roses, scented honeysuckle, *Wisteria* and the many forms of clematis - there are more unusual plants that create an eye-catching display at different times of the year. Try the exotic blooms of *Passiflora,* the passionflower, or the curious parrot's bill, *Clianthus puniceus.* Herald's trumpet, *Beaumaris grandiflora,* produces large, scented white trumpets in spring. For a spectacular summer display, consider the fast-growing coral vine, *Antigonon leptopus,* with its tiny pink or white flowers; or the mass of simple orange-yellow flowers with dark brown centers produced by annual black-eyed Susan, *Thunbergia alata.* There are even climbers offering fall interest, not just the glorious colors of Boston ivy, *Parthenocissus tricuspidata,* but also late-flowering clematis and passifloras.

Right: Climbing and rambling roses can always be relied on to provide a breathtaking summer show of scent and color over walls, fences and pergolas. This is 'Constance Spry', actually a shrub rose with a useful arching habit.

Below: Parthenocissus *are deciduous climbers noted for their end-of-season color. Here,* P. quinquefolia *and* P. parthenocissus *smother a white fence.*

Below: The deciduous climbing hydrangea, Hydrangea petiolaris, *is a highly attractive, woody stemmed climber for walls and strong arches.*

Clematis macropetala
'Lagoon' is a hardy summer-flowering clematis with large semi-double flowers, each one as long as 2in(5cm).

Below: *Wisteria can be trained over wires to create a spectacular covered walkway, providing the site is a sunny one with fertile, well-drained soil.*

The Japanese climbing hydrangea, Hydrangea petiolaris, *has attractive toothed leaves and clusters of small, white fluffy flowers in summer. It is ideal for training up walls.*

Wisteria sinensis 'Caroline', with its delicate oval leaves and hanging racemes of scented double flowers, is perfect for pergolas and leafy walkways.

93

Choosing designer trees

Trees need to be viewed from several different perspectives to appreciate their exciting potential within your garden design. There is the close focus on foliage shape and color, the possibility of blossom, scent, and maybe fruits or berries, too. Then there is the long view; the shape and form of the tree itself, its size and breadth, its growth habit - whether weeping, upright or spreading. Also consider what a particular species can offer your garden as the seasons change; are you looking for spring interest, summer shade or a blaze of color to lift your scheme in the fall? All these factors should influence your final decision. Initially, you will probably be most interested in the overall shape and size of your chosen trees and how they will add height and maturity to your basic framework as described on page 46. Although young trees look very much alike as saplings, each will assume a distinct shape or outline on maturity and it is important to be aware of this before you make your choice. There are tall, narrow trees, such as *Malus baccata* 'Columnaris', which are ideal where space is limited; or small dome-shaped trees to make a focal point or special feature. If you have room, round-headed forms with a spreading habit, such as the Japanese crab apple, *Malus floribunda*, can look superb and provide useful shade. If you plan a group of several trees, try to include contrasting shapes, such as columnar, pyramids or round-headed specimens.

Cytisus battandieri *is a semi-evergreen shrub grown as a small spreading tree. The summer flowers are scented.*

Crataegus laevigata *'Paul's Scarlet', an attractive small tree with glossy dark green leaves and double red blossom in spring.*

Fagus sylvatica *'Dawyck Purple' makes an attractive columnar tree with dark purple foliage. It reaches about 23ft(7m).*

Fagus sylvatica *'Dawyck Gold' adds a stylish splash of gold among a backdrop of green as a special feature.*

Acer grosseri hersii, *the snake's bark maple, is a hardy tree with fine spreading branches of bright green leaves that turn red in fall. The white-striped bark is a special feature.*

Acer platanoides 'Crimson King' *makes a fine spreading tree with deep purple foliage that turns orange in the fall, thus making a fine feature for much of the year.*

Acer platanoides 'Drummondii' *adds a beautiful light effect against darker trees, with its creamy-white edged leaves.*

95

A tree for each season

It is a mistake to consider trees merely as a canopy or backdrop of indistinct greenery within your garden scheme, as their foliage comes in a wonderful rainbow of shades and colors. They need positioning carefully if they are to look harmonious together and with other plant material in the garden. Take seasonal changes into consideration; a blaze of hot pink spring blooms or blossom might sit awkwardly against a tree with bright yellow or golden foliage, for example. Use the more striking colors judiciously as high-lights among greener trees, but take care not to create a lop-sided effect by putting them all to one side. For an interesting backdrop, try combining different greens and creams with the occasional high-light, using trees of differing heights and shapes. Remember, too, that many deciduous trees put on a magnificent display of rich color in the fall. Choose and position such dual-purpose species with care and your garden will be alive with color and interest for most of the year.

Castanea sativa, the sweet chestnut, makes a beautifully spreading tree that needs plenty of space. Yellow fall color.

Planted in the right position, Prunus 'Pink Shell' is only one of many beautiful flowering cherries that will put on a spectacular spring display.

Sorbus aria 'Lutescens' is a good choice for smaller gardens, offering as it does spring, summer and fall interest within a single tree.

Aesculus hippocastanum, *the horse chestnut, is generally chosen for its wide spreading branches, large, dark green leaves, and double flowers in spring.*

Alnus glutinosa *'Imperialis' is a slow-growing variety of the common alder. It has particularly attractive, deeply cut foliage.*

Carpinus betulus *'Frans Fontaine' is a deciduous, round-headed tree with summer catkins and good fall color, followed by winged nuts.*

Betula pendula, *the silver birch, has attractive silver bark. Planting the trees in small groups emphasises the effect of the ghostly silver trunks.*

Trees with a difference

Trees have so much more to offer than simply height, shade and foliage interest. The scent and sight of spring blossom is instantly uplifting and a real boost to the garden after the dark days of winter. But remember that there are summer-flowering trees, too, and many trees with interesting ornamental fruits and berries. Other species have eye-catching bark or colored stems. Position spring-flowering trees where you can view them from the house and enjoy them before the weather is warm enough to spend time in the garden. Summer-flowering varieties, such as the tiny *Magnolia stellata* or *Cladrastis lutea,* are often deliciously scented and these benefit from being placed on the lawn or close by a path or patio where you will be able to enjoy their fragrance. For end of summer interest through into winter, if the birds leave them alone, try to include at least one tree with ornamental berries or fruits, such as the crab apple, *Malus,* the hardy Japanese snowbell, *Styrax japonica,* which has green fruits or, in protected gardens, the tender golden rain tree, *Koelreuteria paniculata,* with its pink lanterns. For winter there are the catkins on the willow, conifers' fascinating variety of cones and the fabulous bark effects of trees such as the silver birch, *Betula pendula,* or red snake-bark maple, *Acer capillipes.* One of the prettiest trees to lose its leaves is the paper, or canoe, birch, *Betula papyrifera,* whose peeling silver bark hangs in tatters to reveal a copper trunk. For all-year interest, include a selection of evergreen trees. *Eucryphia* x *nymansensis* makes an attractive column of glossy dark green leaves, with large white flowers at the end of summer. *Eucalyptus* offers a variety of gray-green foliaged trees that are pleasantly aromatic. And do not forget the wide range of holly cultivars, including pretty variegated effects and bright berries on the female tree.

Left: Moroccan, or pineapple, broom, Cytisus battandieri, *is more of a shrub than a tree, but is ideal for small spaces, where its loose, spreading branches of fresh green foliage are a mass of deliciously pineapple-scented flower spikes from early spring to midsummer.*

Right: Beech trees are generally grown for their attractive shape and interesting foliage color. This Fagus sylvatica 'Dawyck Gold' *has a neat columnar habit and reaches 23ft (7m) - suitable for smaller gardens.*

Above: *The silver birch,* Betula pendula, *makes an elegant, versatile, conical tree, with its attractive, silver-colored bark, spring catkins and yellow fall color.*

Left: *The common oak,* Quercus robur, *is a reliable deciduous tree with an attractive spreading habit. For smaller gardens, the slow-growing Q.r. 'Concordia' reaches 33ft(10m).*

Right: *If you have the space,* Aesculus hippocastanum, *the horse chestnut tree, will reward you with a canopy of large, dark green leaves and flower candles from spring to early summer.*

Choosing specimen trees

Some trees are so eye-catching that they make an unavoidable focal point and must be positioned carefully if you are to make the most of their visual impact. These are trees that need to stand alone, or at least among a suitable background of less dramatic companions, to show them off to best advantage. Within a larger land-scape, for example, a purple beech makes a stunning highlight in a mass of greenery, where two or more trees would create a totally different, rather somber effect. For more modest gardens, there are many smaller specimen trees that can be used successfully to create an exciting focal point, say in the center of a lawn, at the end of a vista or at a particular season of the year. These trees may have attractive foliage, beautiful bark, superb spring blossom, brilliant end-of-summer color, a fine shape or an interesting habit. Some species can offer two or even several of these attributes, making them especially 'garden worthy' and ideal for smaller gardens. Many such trees have been specially developed for this purpose and although they may be expensive to buy, they will amply reward you with a suitably compact habit and special decorative qualities.

Sorbus sp. Harry Smith 12799 *is a good choice for smaller gardens looking for a tree with long season interest.*

Sorbus cashmiriana 'Pink' produces pink flowers in early summer, followed by clusters of berries.

Sorbus x hybrida 'Gibbsii' makes a fine display of cut-edged leaves in summer.

Sorbus 'Chinese Lace' has particularly fine feathery foliage.

Malus 'Butterball' prefers a sunny position, where it makes a fine specimen tree.

Prunus subhirtella 'Flore Pleno' makes a fine display of blossom.

Prunus subhirtella 'Autumnalis Rosea' produces semi-double, pink-flushed flowers in mild winters.

Malus 'Director Moerland' can offer attractive flowers, fine fruits and colorful foliage.

Laburnum x watereri 'Vossii' is grown for its hanging racemes of large yellow flowers in early summer.

Fagus sylvatica 'Aspleniifolia' is a variety of beech distinguished by its deeply cut foliage.

Some choice trees

Flowering cherries, Prunus sp., provide a breathtaking display of blossom in spring, while Japanese maples offer wonderful foliage shape and color. Do not forget trees with interesting fruits: the mountain ash, for example, has pretty feathery foliage graced by sprays of orange or yellow berries, while the useful crab apples, Malus sp., have a fine compact shape, beautiful spring color and attractive, edible fruits. Other small trees that make a fine focal point include the wedding cake tree, Cornus contraversa, and, of course, the spectacular magnolia.

101

Trees as a focal point

A specimen tree needs the right setting if it is to be seen to best advantage. Position it where it will stand out from the crowd and be set against a suitable backdrop that will not obscure its shape or color. There is no point in planting a white-variegated *Cornus alternifolia* 'Argentea' against a white-painted wall or fence, for example; or finding out at the end of summer that your brilliant display of red and purple foliage is completely neutralized by positioning your Japanese maples close to a russet brick wall. Also take particular care when planning the position of some of the special spring-blooming cherries, as their blossom color can be so vivid that it clashes with other flowers and features. Where a tree is to create a special focal point, the center of the lawn or a paved area often gives it suitable prominence. Clipped formal effects in tubs and containers are more likely to be displayed in pairs, on either side of a door or entrance, or flanking a seat. A golden- or silver-leafed tree looks good against a backdrop of dark evergreens, where the contrast will offset the brightness of their leaves, but this would not work with species that have purple or darker foliage. Carefully consider the underplanting of specimen trees, too. A tree with interesting bark should not be partially obscured by an adjacent shrub, clash with a strong color, or detract from other blossom or foliage. Use under-planting to positive effect by coordinating the color of shade-tolerant ground cover with that of your tree. Try to plan something of interest beneath the tree at those times of the year when it is not at its best - perhaps a brave show of spring bulbs in early spring.

Left: Prunus mume 'Beni-chidori' is a deciduous spreading shrub grown as a specimen tree in smaller gardens. It has pointed dark green leaves and scented, deep pink, single flowers that appear on the bare branches in early spring.

Above: Prunus subhirtella 'Pendula Rosea' is a flowering cherry with a weeping habit. Grow it as a focal point where you can appreciate its shape and deep pink spring blossom.

Left: Acer japonicum 'Vitifolium' makes a fine deciduous bushy tree for small gardens. The rounded green leaves turn red in the fall and there are small reddish flowers in spring.

Right: *Oriental poppies beneath* Malus floribunda *add color and interest at ground level. Plan for contrasting or coordinated effects beneath trees with bulbs and shade-tolerant ground cover.*

Below: Laburnum watereri *'Vossi' is a small, relatively shortlived tree grown mainly for its spectacular display of yellow flowers. It is a popular specimen tree for small gardens.*

Ground level interest is important if specimen trees are to be displayed attractively. If the area is unsuitable for plants, cover it with pebbles, gravel or colored chippings.

Right: Acer palmatum atropurpureum *with* Vitis coignetiae *are perfect companions for a fall display, with their striking end-of-summer color. Do make sure that they are planted against a suitable setting.*

Using fruit trees

A tree that produces edible fruits or berries, as well as fine foliage, interesting spring blossom, perhaps striking fall color, too, is certainly a valuable asset in the garden, especially if the plot is a small one. A fruit tree requires very little extra maintenance: perhaps a little pruning and an occasional spray against insects. If you only have room for one tree and want to make a feature of it, choose a variety that not only has a good and interesting shape, but one that is self-pollinating and has been specially bred for its disease resistance and high crop yield. For cottage-style gardens you might consider the crab apple, rowan or quince, whose fruits make a fine display at the end of summer - or a tasty jam or jelly if you prefer. Fruit trees can be trained to create a decorative feature, as well as a productive one; intertwine the branches to create arches and tunnels or, where space is really restricted, train them along wires against a wall, fence or trellis in fan and espalier shapes. Larger gardens might include a group of several fruit trees, say, a plum or a cherry and one or two varieties of pear, like a miniature orchard. When choosing a position for a fruiting tree, allow it sufficient space to develop properly. It is also a good idea to keep it away from any paved areas, as dropping fruit and bird lime can make a mess on the ground.

Ballerina apple trees have been specially developed for small gardens. A single vertical stem produces a heavy crop of fruit.

Bush apple 'Gala' (here grafted onto a M27 rootstock) is a crisp, juicy dessert apple with good flavor. It is free-fruiting, which makes it ideal for small gardens.

Left: *Old-fashioned, two-dimensional cordon and espalier techniques for fruit trees mean that they can be grown in the minimum of space - even around this Victorian curved wall in an old walled garden.*

Bush cherry 'Morello' (here on Colt rootstock) is one of few fruits that will grow better out of direct sunshine. It produces edible fruits for making cherry brandy or for bottling.

Container-grown trees can be planted at any time, as long as the ground is not frozen.

Above: *The morello* cherry, Prunus cerasus *'Austera', will grow on a wall facing away from the sun, yet produces a fine display of spring blossom and summer fruit.*

Above: *If you have space for a range of fruit trees, try to include a plum. The fruits are a favorite with wasps, but make delicious jellies and pies.*

Below: *An old apple tree, its spreading branches in full bloom, is a wonderful sight and the perfect setting for a meal beneath the sweetly scented blossom.*

Index to Plants

Page numbers in **bold** indicate major text references. Page numbers in *italics* indicate captions and annotations to photographs. Other text entries are shown in normal type.

Credits

The majority of the photographs featured in this book have been taken by Neil Sutherland and are © Colour Library Books. The publishers wish to thank the following photographers for providing additional photographs, credited here by page number and position on the page, i.e. (B)Bottom, (T)Top, (C)Center, (BL)Bottom left, etc.

Eric Crichton: Copyright page, 16(TR), 17(TR,BR), 20(BR), 25(TL), 28(TR,BR), 29(T,BL), 32(BR), 33(BR) 36(TL,BL), 37(T,BL,BR), 40(BL), 41(BR), 44(R), 48(B), 49(BR), 53(T,BR), 56(B), 57(BR), 67(TC,TR,BR), 73(T), 76(BL), 85(TL), 87(L), 89(TR), 91(BR), 93(BL), 105(BR)
John Glover: 10, 16(BL,BR), 17(BL), 20(TR), 24(TL,BL,BR), 25(B), 29(BR), 32(TL,BL), 33(TR), 36(CR), 40(TL,BR), 41(T), 44(BL), 45(T,BL,BR), 49(L), 53(BL), 57(BL), 63, 65(TR,BR), 71(TR), 73(BR), 75(T), 76(TR,BR), 83(TR,BR), 85(TR), 86(BL), 91(TR), 92(L,BR), 98(T,BR), 99(L,TR,BR), 102(TR), 103(BL, BR), 104(BL), 105(TC,TR)
Jerry Harpur (Harpur Picture Library) 20(TR, Designer Felicity Mullen), 21(BL, BR), 52(BL,BR)
Clive Nichols: Half-title, 11, 33(BL), 41(BL), 48(TL), 49(TR), 56(TL), 57(TL), 62, 69(TR), 70(BL,BR), 71(BL,BR), 79(T), 92-3(TC), 102(TL,BL), 103(TR)
Don Wildridge: 25(TR)

Acknowledgments

The publishers would like to thank Bridgemere Garden World, near Nantwich in Cheshire, for providing plants and photographic facilities during the production of this book; thanks are particularly due to John Ravenscroft and Rosalind Harrington. The garden models were prepared by June Carter and Stuart Watkinson of Ideas into Print.